1974 by the Fels Center of Government,
University of Pennsylvania
All rights reserved
usly in Canada by George J. McLeod Limited,
Toronto
in the United States of America

Power and the Structure

of Society

f Congress Cataloging in Publication Data
James S
er and the structure of society.
s lectures on public policy analysis)
ography: p.
ower (Social sciences)   2. Bureaucracy.
rations.   4. Civil rights.   I. Title.

63   301.5'92   73–14727
393–05503–5
393–09327–1 (pbk.)

3 4 5 6 7 8 9 0

Copyright

Published simultan

Prin

Pow

FELS LECTURES ON PUBLIC POLICY ANALYSIS

The Limits of Organization / KENNETH J. ARROW
Power and the Structure of Society / JAMES S. COLEMAN
The Moon and the Ghetto / RICHARD R. NELSON
Guido Calabresi / TRAGIC CHOICES

Library
Colema
Po
(F
Bi
1.
3. Cor
II. Seri
HM136
ISBN o
ISBN o

W · W

To Zdislawa Walaszek, whose concern
with power and control parallels my own.

Contents

Preface   9

1   EMERGENCE OF NEW PERSONS   11

2   SEPARATION OF POWER FROM ITS SOURCE   33

3   RESTITUTION   55

4   LEARNING TO LIVE WITH NEW PERSONS   85

References   107

Index   109

Preface

IN PREPARING the four lectures of which this book consists, I wanted to create, with broad strokes, a sketch of the emergent structure of modern western society as I see it. The lectures constitute a brief introduction to a more detailed and painstaking effort to lay out a theoretical structure useful for the analysis of modern society.

Implicit in the aims of this enterprise is the belief that we are at a stage in social development in which a theory of social structure is particularly important: we have sufficient physical knowledge to control much of our natural environment, but future social development depends on our self-conscious shaping of social structure. The ability to do that depends on a much fuller understanding of the functioning of society than we have currently attained, understanding which appropriately takes the form of social theory.

These lectures do not constitute such a theory, but give only a glimpse of the directions the theory will take. However, I believe they show as well some of the directions that restructuring of society may appropriately take, and some directions for fruitful research into the structure of society.

I am grateful to Julius Margolis, Director of the Fels Center of Government, for inviting me to give the second annual set of lectures, and thus providing an opportunity for an earlier exposition of these ideas than I would otherwise have had. I am grateful to several persons for comments and criticisms which aided in revision of the lectures: Gudmund Hernes, John Markoff, Aaron Wildavsky, and most especially

Sasha Weitman. Professor Weitman's detailed critique, going far beyond the obligations of friendship, greatly improved the resulting manuscript—although I am sure that neither he nor my other commentators would be fully in accord with the monograph that has resulted.

1

EMERGENCE OF NEW PERSONS

THE COMMON-SENSE WAY of
viewing society is as a vast network or organization of persons. Social scientists as well use that conception, though they
have introduced another, by describing society and social
organization as composed of "roles" and "role relations." This
depiction of society as consisting of persons occupying roles
has, I suspect, been of some value for understanding the functioning of society. But there seems nowhere to exist, neither
among social scientists nor among others who discuss these
matters, the recognition that the society has changed over the
past few centuries, in the very structural elements of which
it is composed.

A sensitive indicator of this change may be found in law,
because law (along with politics) is the practicing profession
for which social organization is the central field of operations.
Thus legal theory must face problems of social organization
as they arise, while academic social theory need not deal with
reality, but only with the constructions of it in academic
journals. And especially must law confront new social inventions when they arise, insofar as these inventions have an
impact on other aspects of society.

Thus it should occasion some reassurance to social scientists to find throughout western society that in fact the law
does conceive of social organization as built around *persons*:
their actions, the events that befall them, their relations to
other persons, their interests, and even their intentions. Obviously law has found it both necessary and possible to carry
out its practice from a conceptual framework involving *persons, actions, events, resources, interests, rights,* and *duties.*

But it should be somewhat unsettling to social scientists
to discover that law does not mean quite the same thing by
"person" as you or I do. In law there are, in fact, two major

kinds of persons: physical persons of the sort that you and I know, indeed are, which the law calls "natural persons," and "juristic persons."[1] These "juristic persons" are intangible entities which none of us natural persons has ever seen. They include what we commonly think of as corporations, along with many other entities: churches, certain clubs, trade associations, labor unions, professional associations, towns, and others. In law, these persons must be treated somewhat differently from natural persons: they have no fixed life span, and thus may exist in perpetuity, they have no corpus, and thus cannot be physically imprisoned (though they can be punished in other ways, including death, a sentence not infrequently imposed by judges), they have no intrinsic capability of acting, and so must act through agents in the form of natural persons.

One might ask, to all this, "So what's new?" The answer is that the modern corporation, the juristic person formed for specific purposes by its members, is new, and its presence has created societies with different structural foundations than those which existed in the past. Until about the fifteenth century, law had no place for juristic persons of this sort, able to freely engage in transactions. The only corporate bodies were those—the manor, the guild, the village—which wholly contained their members, which had full authority and responsibility over them, and which had fixed relations to subordinate and superordinate corporate bodies in a hierarchical structure. But several centuries earlier the law had begun to run into difficult problems, because a new sort of creature was growing up for which no legal niche existed. This crea-

---

[1] It is, in fact, a fallacy to identify "natural persons" with physical individuals, for there is only an approximate correspondence between the two. A natural person is a legal construct, implying certain rights and responsibilities. Minors, the mentally incompetent, and some others are not natural persons before the law. In the fourteenth century in Europe, there were many classes of persons who were not regarded as natural persons before the law. Maitland lists monks, jews, serfs as physical persons who in England were not natural persons before the law.

ture might be termed a "free corporate actor," in contrast to those medieval corporate bodies which had a fixed place and function in a rigid organic structure.[2] I will use several terms interchangeably in referring to this new creature: juristic person, corporate actor, corporation.

Over a period of centuries, it became clear that this creature functioned in many ways like a natural person, with which the law was familiar. The most fruitful way the law found for dealing with this entity was to treat it as a person, a person with certain special characteristics; a person not born of woman but of legislative bodies, but nevertheless a person in the eyes of the law. This has turned out to be a very fruitful solution indeed, so much so that juristic persons have had an enormous population growth, far surpassing the population explosion of real persons. Over a century ago, in 1857, a judge in Illinois said: "It is probably true that more corporations were created by the legislature of Illinois at its last session than existed in the whole civilized world at the commencement of the present century."[3]

In this first chapter, I want to trace something of the history of these new elements in society, the *corporate actors* as I will often call them, and then in the subsequent chapters indicate some of the implications for social organization and for social policy of this new social structure in which these juristic persons play such an important part. But at this point it may be helpful if I give a foretaste of these implications. The implications have largely to do with *interests* and *rights*: the interests and rights of natural persons and of corporate actors, and how they interrelate. The relation is a complex one, for there is a symbiosis between natural persons and corporate actors. Nevertheless, each person before the law, whether a natural person or a corporate actor, has interests and rights. And the interests of corporate actors are

[2] See Gierke (1934) and Weber (1954) for descriptions of the character of these corporate bodies of the middle ages.
[3] Quoted by Maitland (p. xii) in translator's introduction to Gierke (1900).

not merely an aggregate of the interests of their members (or employees, or agents, or founders, or managers). Nor are they a direct reflection of the interests of any natural persons. In the construction of a humane society, it is necessary to look carefully at the relation between interests of corporate actors and those of natural persons who stand in various relations to those corporate actors. Thus the overall aim of this book will be to examine this emergent social structure with which we find ourselves. The purpose will be as well to ask what are the particular problems to which social policy must address itself if this social structure is to best serve the ends of natural persons.

To simplify the story of the emergence of corporate actors, there were three kinds of problems that began to arise beginning around the twelfth century in Europe. One involved *churches*, another involved *towns*, and a third involved *kings*.

Churches

To turn to the churches first, it was the practice in Germany in the Middle Ages for a landowner to build a church on his land, to put a priest in the church, and to have that church used by those persons attached to him, as a kind of extension of his household.[4] All this was in accord with the hierarchical social structure of those times. And it was probably a carry-over from pre-Christian religious practices in Europe. But then problems arose. The priest of the church began to argue, successfully, that the landowner no longer held full rights over the church and the land which surrounded it. One of the first rights to be withdrawn was the right to have slaves that were confirmed in the church work the land associated with the church, or to do work for the church as slaves. Slowly, the rights of the landowner began to dwindle, and he became the "patron" of the church, at one

---

[4] See Pollock and Maitland (1898), Vol. 1, p. 499.

remove from control over it; and as patron, his rights further declined.

As these rights left the patron and as the church began to be independent of his control, a new question arose: To whom *did* the rights belong? Not the priest, because the priest could die, or could move to another church. The matter became increasingly important, because as these churches grew in independence from their patron, and as they came to have independent sources of income, the rights involved became more than merely negative ones. They began to involve commodities and resources, land above all things, which could be bought and sold. But who was their owner? In whom did the rights reside, now that they had left the patron?

The law found this a very difficult problem to deal with, for it had no immediate answer. A number of devices were used. One was to declare the "four walls of the church" the owner, but this was not very successful. Another, which now appears a desperate measure but was used seriously for a period of time, was to declare the saint for whom the church was named as the owner. Thus many centuries after their deaths, St. Peter and St. Paul and St. James became extensive property owners. The law had found a solution. When property associated with St. Paul's church was transferred, the seller would be St. Paul, while the guardian of St. Paul's property, who acted to protect his interests, was the priest currently installed in St. Paul's church.

It began to be apparent that this practice would serve, and even further that the saint was performing no crucial function other than having his name used, serving as the person who owned, bought, and sold property. Thus slowly the practice grew in law of naming the church itself as owner. By the thirteenth century in England, not only had this practice developed, but also a theory about the *kind* of person the church was. For example, the church was regarded as an infant, to be protected by law against the "guardian's" negligence. A *juristic person* had developed, independent of any particular natural persons (though continually under the guardianship of a priest), having many of the rights in law held by real persons. This did not mean, of course, that all the problems were solved: Could the church, for example, be apprehended and held liable for criminal action? What happened if the guardianship fell vacant? Who was qualified to speak for the interests of this new legal person? How were conflicts among those who controlled the church's interests resolved?

Towns

At about the same time that these ecclesiastical matters were creating legal precedent a different sort of juristic person was developing in England and on the Continent, around geographic communities. In England, the boroughs were differentiating themselves from villages, and in the thirteenth and fourteenth centuries were coming to have a corporate character not possessed by the counties, nor by the hundreds (a quasi-corporate group of Germanic origin), nor by the villages. But what created this? It might be argued that it was the king's actions, in levying fines and rents against the boroughs. The fines were not always borne corporately, but sometimes severally by the separate burgesses themselves, so the idea of corporateness had not yet developed fully. Nevertheless, one of the two forces which were giving the boroughs a unity of action were these actions taken against them as a unit by the king, by a lord, by a creditor. The other, and perhaps more powerful, force was the rights that were conferred by the king to the boroughs in their charters, rights that required them to be treated before the law as corporate bodies. These rights were often in tolls and franchises. The borough not only took tolls, and was paid for franchises, it could also sell the rights it owned. In 1225, for example, the "burgesses of Nottingham" let certain tolls to "the burgesses of Retford" for perpetual rent at twenty marks, a transaction in effect between two single persons. Correspondingly, the law had to recognize that such a transaction had taken place, that it *could* take place. The only convenient way found to recognize this was through the idea of juristic persons. With this idea, much of the legal apparatus that was used for natural persons could be directly applied.

Kings

The third legal problem that began to emerge concerned kings. This arose somewhat later than the others, about the sixteenth century, and only in England. It gave rise to a new concept in English law, the "corporation sole." What was the problem?

One way to show it is by example. Edward IV had sold some land of the Duchy of Lancaster, which had been acquired by an earlier king. This resulted in a suit in court over the legality of the act. The legality was questioned for one reason only: the king was nine years old when he sold the lands. One set of lawyers argued that this invalidated the action, since the king was a minor, and minors could not buy and sell on their own account, i.e. did not have the full status of persons before the law. The king's councillors argued, however, that the action was in fact law, and for a special reason: the king had two bodies, the physical body and the body politic. The "body politic," who they argued has acted in this case, knew no minority, no infirmity, no old age, knew neither birth nor death. In English law, there developed a controversy over the king's "two bodies," a controversy which led often in mystical directions as the characteristics of this second intangible body were described and extolled. To a modern reader these arguments often have the same unreal flavor as the medieval arguments about how many angels could stand on the head of a pin. But these arguments were of serious social consequence. They led to an explicit separation of "The Crown" from the particular king who was the current possessor of the Crown. It led to a separation of the idea of the monarchy from the particular monarch. It allowed the Parliament, during the rebellion against Charles I in 1642, to engage in what would be otherwise inexplicable: to strike a medallion showing the visage of Charles I while they were in rebellion against him. It allowed kings to be beheaded without the monarchy falling. Some legal historians argue that its absence in France did not allow the monarchy to survive a fallen monarch.[5]

The idea of the "corporation sole" in English law did not have the social necessity behind it, the emergent social forces, that the other sources of the idea of corporation had, as evidenced by its absence on the Continent. Some English historians, in fact, deplore the existence of the concept of corporation sole, and see it as wholly unnecessary in English law.[6] It is instructive to see why this is so. There were problems, such as the one illustrated in the case of a nine-year-old Edward IV, but they were not persistent. A king had always been able to engage in acts as a king, with special rights in law. He was at the apex of the secular hierarchy, as the Pope was at the apex of the ecclesiastical one, and those hierarchies were more or less recognized in law as juristic persons. The law had little problem with them because one physical person was at their head, and he was at the head of the whole social organism. Thus, his actions were the actions of that social organism. There was no question of an aggregate forming into a single entity to be treated as an entity rather than an aggregate. These problems of "aggregateness" or "corporateness" arose with the boroughs.

Nevertheless, the development of the concept of the corporation sole is a useful indication of the growing separation in social organization of the natural person and certain juristic persons. This separation is most necessary when the nat-

[5] See Kantorowicz (1957).
[6] See Pollock and Maitland (1898), Chap. VI.

ural persons making up the corporate body are several, as in
a borough, rather than one, as with the Crown. But in either
case, the separation was occurring in a variety of different
ways.

One of these ways led to another concept in English law
which had different social forces behind it, the concept of
trust. It is instructive to see its origin in English law. It was
borrowed from Lombardy, where men could not make a will
in the usual sense, but could only transfer property to an
intermediary (a "trustee"), with more or less explicit instruc-
tions about its disposal. Englishmen of the fourteenth century with some property seized upon this device and modified
it to their own use.[7] Their problem was this: for personal
property, that is, property other than land, men could make
a testament, and dispose of their goods upon death through
that testament, according to their own will. But the strict
primogeniture of England made this impossible for land.
Land must be passed to the first-born son, and in being so
passed, was subject to taxes levied by the lord, or other kinds
of levies, in some cases reverting wholly to the lord. The idea
of a trust, an *inter vivos* trust, was introduced to thwart the
lord and give power to the landholder. It operated this way:
the landholder conveyed his land to a set of trustees, who
held it to his use during his lifetime; and he could tell them
what to do with it after his death. It was very much like the
inter vivos trust of today, which has been resuscitated not to
escape inheritance taxes (the modern state is more cunning
and more powerful than the gentry of fourteenth-century
England), but to escape the lawyers themselves, and especially their fees.

The crucial element in this fourteenth-century trust, from
the point of view of the later strength it exhibited, was the
fact that the land was conveyed to a *set* of persons, not to
one alone. Thus, if one died, he could be replaced, and the
set would continue in perpetuity if necessary. No inheritance

[7] See Maitland (1904), p. 10 ff.

taxes were ever due the lord, because although one member of the trust might die, the trust *as an entity* did not die. As its number diminished, it might be brought back to full strength by additions. But in essence what had happened as a by-product of this device was the creation of something that is almost a juristic person, an entity which can hold property in trust for another, but was not itself a full person before the law. It is unnecessary to describe the power that this instrument came to have in the heyday of capitalism, particularly in America. It constituted a means of amassing, holding, and putting to use enormous amounts of economic power. It is perhaps less well known that this same instrument in seventeenth-century England came to be the means through which religious liberty developed. The Nonconformists and the Catholic churches could not have been formed as corporations, because that meant a conferring by the state of special privileges through a charter, as well as special obligations to the state. The established church certainly had sufficient strength to prevent such explicit recognition by the state, and the Noncomformists had no wish to incur obligations to the state. The corporation at this time was still too tightly connected to the residue of the hierarchical structure of society, still too much a creature of the state. Only the trust had the status of being recognized by the courts as having almost the rights of ownership through the rights of trusteeship, which came to be nearly the same thing, yet not requiring a charter from the state, nor even explicit recognition by the state. The trust had just the right degree of being to escape the compressing strictures of the state, and yet offer a shield of legal protection for a certain set of activities that required resources. If these activities were religious, it provided an avenue for escape from the established religion—an avenue which did not exist on the Continent, where trusts had not been able to develop. If the activities were economic, it provided an avenue for economic freedom, freedom from too great state interference.

During this time, a new set of legal concepts was being discovered in England and on the Continent: Roman law, which had lain dormant for some centuries, was being studied by legal scholars, and was bringing in old ideas to provide the basis for new law. One of the most important of these was the Roman concept of *universitas*, which was something more than the German *Gesellschaft*, something more than the English *association*. The *universitas* in Roman law was treated as a single entity, rather than an aggregate of men. It could be applied to a college (colleges at Oxford and Cambridge were early English entities to which the term *universitas* was applied), or to a body of men joined around another purpose, such as the baristers and jurists at Lincoln's Inn in London. And the concept of "fictional person" was found in Roman law and canon law (that is, Roman church law), a single entity in the eyes of the law, yet a fictional one. The idea of *universitas*, and the idea of a fictional person before the law, began to give a conceptual base to the social facts that were developing. Thus the structure of legal ideas which had preceded the Middle Ages in Roman law was being revived and modified to accommodate the new social forces emerging with the waning of the Middle Ages.

In all this, it is most useful to see the law not as a social force, but as a kind of cumulative record of social forces which bring it into effect. What was happening in this period of time, beginning around the eleventh century, and continuing to the present, was a breakdown of the hierarchical structure of society of which the Middle Ages was composed. To see this, it is only necessary to examine carefully what was new in the concept of the fictional person or the juristic person or the corporation. What was *not* new was the possibility of an entity other than a natural person owning property or holding rights. Roman cities had public property, as had cities long before, in the form of stadia, theaters, and other public buildings. Towns and villages in medieval England had commons, which were held by the town and used in common by the townspeople. The central Roman church, at the apex of its hierarchy, held property, and had extensive rights. Kings, long before the concept of "corporation sole," had special rights which let property pass directly from king to successor, without the concept of "inheritance." What was not new was the concept of these social entities *as* entities. The basic unit of settlement and of protection for Germanic tribes much earlier than the twelfth century was the "hundred"; and there were guilds of tradesmen throughout the Middle Ages. The manor in England consisted of all the persons bound to the manor, who recognized themselves as such. The church existed as a social entity, as did its various organs, councils of bishops and the like.

What *was* new was the idea that certain entities had rights to engage in transactions on their own, so to speak— rights to determine on their own what they would own, buy, and sell. It was in *this* sense that social entities became juristic persons. They were no longer fully bound by the hierarchical structure, no longer constrained in the set of relations in which they engaged, no longer confined to a fixed set of relationships. Local churches could enter into transactions on their own, not at the will of the patron, nor at the will of the central church authority. Boroughs could use their tolls and their franchises as they liked, through the will of the burgesses and not the king. And as this freedom developed further, men who were joined together for reasons other than religion or residence in the same borough could do the same. The joint-stock corporation is one culmination of this; the clubs, associations, and other organizations, joined together for purposes of profit or not, could come to have many of the legal rights enjoyed by persons: rights of ownership, rights of transaction, but particularly rights to act under their own will, to establish and break relationships, to make contracts. In effect, what was created with the growth of corporation was a flexibility in the structure of society, a source of continual modification and change in that structure, change coming from below, through the combined force of many men acting as one and treated in law as one.

What was new for corporate bodies was in fact exactly the same thing that had been new for many individuals only a short time before. For many individuals were themselves just coming into recognition as persons before the law, with rights to buy, sell, and hold property, acting on their own will rather than as a chattel or villein to a lord. These new persons before the law were different in a fundamental way from the subjects they had replaced. Their relations, their activities, their contracts, their property were not prescribed for them by the position of their birth, but rather were open to change at their own discretion. In short, they had attained the same freedom of action, the same possibility of making and breaking relations, of mobility in a social structure, the same recognition as independent persons, that corporate bodies were to attain some years later.

This change is an especially interesting one to examine, because it constituted a wholly different construction of society from that of the Middle Ages. Medieval society was composed of an articulated hierarchy of subordinate entities, each with its place and function. Medieval political theory conceived of that hierarchy as an organic unity, sometimes using direct analogies between the parts of society and the physical parts of an individual. For example, Gierke says:

In Church and Empire the Total Body is a manifold and graduated system of Partial Bodies, each of which, though itself a Whole, necessarily demands connexion with the larger whole. It has a final cause of its own, and consists of Parts which it procreates and dominates, and which in their turn are Wholes. Between the highest Universality or "All-Community" and the absolute Unity of the individual man, we find a series of intermediating units, in each of which lesser and lower units are comprised and combined. Medieval theory endeavoured to establish a definite scheme descriptive of this articulation, and the graduated hierarchy of the Church served as a model for a parallel system of temporal groups. When it comes to particulars, there will be differences between different schemes; but it is common to see five organic groups placed above the individual and the family: namely village, city, province, nation or kingdom, empire: but sometimes several of these grades will be regarded as one.[8]

This articulated structure as seen by medieval theory was wholly hierarchical in form, and relations between parts of that structure were relations between superordinate and subordinate, not between coequals.[9] Historians of social theory have described the organismic theories of the Middle Ages, and the anthropomorphic imagery that could be found in those theories. They have ordinarily rejected, and sometimes scoffed at, the organismic conceptions. But they are wrong in doing so. The social theory of the Middle Ages *was* appropriately descriptive of the social structure. It was not descriptive of society before that time, nor of society since, but it did describe that social structure.

The breakup of that structure came through a kind of pincers movement of the two ends against the middle. The apex of the hierarchy, monarch, gained in power and in function, and at the other extreme, the individual did as well. The fixed intermediary structure relating the individual to the monarch declined in strength. Two political movements, and two theories, replaced ideas of society as an organism: the theory of the absolute power of the state, and the theory of natural rights of the individual. These were in direct conflict, but they were also directly opposed to the

[8] See Gierke (1900), p. 21.
[9] Historians of medieval society differ in their attribution of hierarchy to the social structure. But this seems to be a disagreement of what descriptive term to use more than a disagreement of facts. What is generally accepted is that (1) a corporate body fully contained the persons within it, who had no recognized existence outside it; (2) the corporate bodies were related to one another in an inclusive relation, one a part of the other, rather than a contractual relation; but (3) the origins of these bodies were local, and developed from below, rather than from above; and (4) most real power existed at the level of the manor, the effective landholding entity, and kings were weak. It was only later that the power of the king increased.

medieval conception of every part in its place in the larger whole.

As the social organism slowly broke down, as the king or the state gained in power and as individuals gained in power, becoming free persons rather than the smallest unit in the social organism, a new set of intermediary entities emerged between the individual and the state, filling the power void slowly being created. Natural persons needed vehicles through which they could express and use their new-found power. The result was the modern corporation—self-governing entities, capable of willing and acting, capable of making and breaking relations, governed from below rather than above. They arose in the most traditional of forms, in the churches and the landed communities, but they then spread to purposive associations of all sorts.

This early emergence of corporate actors was merely the foretaste of what was to come. In England, the precedent for charters from the crown outside the medieval hierarchy was provided by the early charters to boroughs, as I have already described. Then, as England became in subsequent centuries a trading nation, men had interests in combining forces to make possible large trading enterprises. The East India Company, which for a time in effect constituted the government of India, is the best-known example. Colonizing enterprises, such as the companies which settled Virginia, were chartered under the same principle, with the same freedom to engage in a wide range of activities.[10]

The matter can be summed up in this way: in the Middle Ages, productive enterprise involved land, and populations were relatively stable in size. The Mediterranean was con-

[10] These companies and others which existed under early charters had far fewer freedoms than have subsequent corporations chartered in the nineteenth century. It was probably important to their effective freedom that they operated outside the boundaries of England. A similar situation prevailed for the Medici bankers of Florence, whose operations were spread over Europe. It may be that the internationalization of corporations in modern society will similarly free them from control by an increasingly powerful modern state.

trolled from its southern shores by hostile tribes, and the North Sea by hostile Vikings, making Europe effectively landlocked, restricting trade, and limiting enterprise to agriculture. For that period, a peculiarly rigid form of social structure, feudalism, was possible, with a fixed hierarchy in which each man was not free to engage in economic (or even social) relations other than those which fixed him within that hierarchy. But then as the seas opened up, as population increased, and as commerce became important, that fixed structure was no longer viable. Two things happened. First, men themselves began to break out of their fixed estates, began to have rights to appear before the king's court, rights to make contracts on their own; became, in effect, persons before the law with a certain set of rights (elevated by seventeenth-century philosophers to the status of "natural rights") to engage in a variety of activities at their own pleasure. But second, and as a direct consequence of this fragmentation of the feudal structure, a different kind of intermediate organization arose in society: a corporate actor which had, under charter from the king, a variety of rights to free and expansive action. This new corporate actor became the instrument through which men could jointly exercise their new-found rights.

Such flexible units, which could be born and die, expand and contract, move into new arenas of action, and engage in market transactions, came to constitute an ideal organizational frame through which technological developments could bring about social change. The industrial revolution began and developed in England, and it did so because this reconstruction of society, which had proceeded more rapidly in England than in Western Europe, gave the organizational instrument. The concept of the corporation, created for a purpose, untied from land but vested with the economic power of several men, and many of the legal rights of a natural person, had both the potential power and the freedom of action to enable it to engage in trade, banking, manu-

facture, shipping, and all the other activities that make up
an industrial economy.

The transformation of society, from one in which corporate actors wholly contain the persons who are their members, to one in which the corporate actors contain only the
resources vested in them by their members or owners and the
services of their agents, has occurred more rapidly in some
arenas than in others. It began first in economic activity,
with the business corporation. Even there, the family-owned
or closely held corporation (which were prevalent in most
countries other than the United States before World War II)
had this form only on the side of its employees or agents, and
not on the side of its owners. Nonpurposive corporations, into
which persons are born, such as the family, the village or
town, and the nation, have been the last to show this transformation. But more and more, with increased mobility of
persons among such bodies, even these corporate bodies
have come to take on the characteristic form of no longer
containing their members, but only contain the resources
vested in them by their members. The nation-state is a special case, for the political philosophy of natural rights developed to give a conceptual basis for the belief that sovereignty resides in individual persons, who then vest a portion
of that sovereignty in the state as a corporate actor. This
conception is reflected by the shift of the individual from a
subject to a *citizen*. It is a conceptual change that first characterized the New World, was somewhat later in England,
and still later on the Continent. It is a change that is even
now not complete, for with every generation in western
society, the individual person's embeddedness in the state is
less, and the conception of the individual person as the legit-
imate owner of ultimate rights is greater.

Altogether, this transformation of society has been greatest for the intermediary bodies to which persons are connected, least for the one closest to him and the one farthest,
the family and the nation. The prototype is the modern bu-

reaucratic corporation, and its development has hastened the transformation of society in other institutional areas.

The concept of the modern corporation has not been static; major changes occurred with the evolution of the principle of limited liability, which explicitly separates the corporate property from the owners' individual properties, and protects the latter from liabilities of the corporation. Neither has the position of corporate actors in society been static. In America, in particular, corporations grew with remarkable speed. In part, this was due to an historical happenstance. In the U.S. Constitution, the right to charter corporate bodies, whether they were towns or other corporations, was left to the states. Each state drew up its own laws of incorporation, and these laws differed. Many state legislatures were eager to see new corporate enterprises located within their boundaries, and thus made the task of incorporation an extremely simple and attractive one. The result was that in the nineteenth century, the number of corporations in American society grew enormously. As one observer stated in 1894, describing the change in the state of Michigan:

Before 1850 [in Michigan], we had about forty-five mining corporations, seven or more railroad corporations, a few banking corporations, several plank-road corporations, and a few of a miscellaneous character; all, of course, under special charters [with the exception of religious corporations].

General laws to the number of one hundred and fifty-six have been passed from time to time since 1850 for incorporating almost every kind of lawful business and association, and the result has been that we now have [in Michigan] about eight thousand corporations which are organized under those general laws, divided as follows: manufacturing and mercantile, twenty-five hundred; mining, thirteen hundred and twenty-eight; railroad, seventy-nine; street railway, one hundred and thirty-two; transportation, one hundred and twenty-three, state banking, one hundred and fifty-nine; charitable, two hundred and forty-eight; improvement, seventy-seven; miscellaneous, twenty-eight hundred and eighty-two.

To this great number of domestic corporations must be added one hundred national banking corporations, and a large and not ascertainable number of foreign corporations . . . which do business in this state by its express permission.[11]

This growth of corporations and ease of incorporation differed from one part of the western world to another. It was greatest in America, next in England, next in Western Europe, and next in Eastern Europe. As one traveled east from America, the control of the state over those activities within it increased; the concession of corporate rights from the state was more difficult to come by, and more circumscribed. Yet throughout America and Europe the reconstruction of society occurred; these flexible and mobile actors came to constitute elements of the social structure which developed. They constituted the vehicle for economic development, and the institutional structure able to sustain a political democracy.

But this reconstruction of society, this social invention which brought into society a new set of structural elements, brought with it some problems. It is to these problems that I will turn in the next chapter.

[11] From Presidential Address, "Corporations in Michigan," Alfred Russell, Publications of Michigan Political Science Association, No. 2, p. 97, 1894. Quoted in Davis (1905).

2

SEPARATION OF POWER FROM ITS SOURCE

THE FIRST CHAPTER has described the early stages of a transformation of society which occurred over a period of centuries. The period started with an organic structure in which every man and every corporate body had its fixed station, with each man totally contained within that corporate body which had authority over him and responsibility for him. It culminated in a fluid structure consisting of mobile persons acting under their own will, and free to form corporate bodies which were also subject to their will. Thus the oppression of the pyramidal structure of the Middle Ages was removed, and the state which succeeded it was forced to share its power with the newly free persons and their creatures, the self-governing corporate bodies.

But solution of one problem brings another in its wake. The past century has seen these corporate actors grow to immense size and immense power. What was once a hard shell of protection for men, shielding them from the state and giving them the strength of collective action, has come to be something different. It still provides that protection, that shield from the state, but it has come to develop power of its own. The nature of that power, the way that power came to be garnered by the corporate actors, and some of the consequences of the power are the topics of this chapter.

The Marginality of Natural Persons to Corporate Actors

One of the central elements of the new corporate actors of modern society is that persons in them are replaceable. The rigid corporate bodies of the Middle Ages were constructed of persons as component parts, and persons were wholly contained within them. The new corporate actors had a different relation to persons. As *members* or *owners* of a corporation, persons invested resources in it to be used for the corporation's purposes, with the hope of receiving a return on that investment. As *employees* or *agents* of a corporation, persons performed certain services for the corporation in return for compensation paid from the corporation's resources. But any natural person, whether member, owner, employee, agent, or in some other relation to the corporate actor, was replaceable. The component parts of the corporate actor were positions or roles, and the only function of persons was to carry out the activities belonging to the positions they held. The corporate actor came to have the form described by Weber as bureaucracy, a form in which the component parts are not persons but positions.

This structure constituted a major aspect of the freedom newly available to persons: no longer the component parts of corporations and no longer wholly contained within them, persons were free to leave the employ or the membership of the corporate body, with the position they vacated soon occupied by another.

Thus in this transformation of society, persons no longer were the building blocks of which corporate bodies were constructed, no longer the elements of the corporate body. "Positions" became those elements, and persons merely filled positions, with one person substitutable for another.

This transformation has only in recent years been fully felt as the new corporate structure has replaced the old in nearly all activities of life. Its consequence is enormous: there are now two parallel structures of relations coexisting in society—the structure of relations among natural persons, and the structure of relations among these corporate actors that employ the services or resources of persons. These two structures are connected through the symbiosis described above. But they are two different structures of relations, consisting of two different sets of actors (natural persons and corporate actors), with neither type of actor contained by the other or an intrinsic element of the other.

In this circumstance, a condition can arise which is wholly new to society: one person can suffer a loss of power without another person receiving a corresponding gain. The sum total of power among persons in society is no longer constant, because of the new set of actors which have power in themselves—power that resides in the corporate actor and does not accrue to any person connected to that corporate actor. This is a difficult but important distinction. Marx's failure to make it led to the central flaw in his analysis of capitalism, for failing to make it, he located corporate power in the hands of persons, the capitalists, "as a class." The point is that the power held by corporate bodies (whether business corporations, trade unions, governmental bodies, or still another form) is in the hands of no person, but resides in the corporate actor itself. How this occurs I will describe in the succeeding pages of this chapter; but before that, it is necessary to suggest the social problems that this structure can generate.

It is possible, in such a structure, for the sum total of power held by all natural persons to continually decrease, with a corresponding increase in that held by corporate actors. If this has in fact happened, it constitutes a loss to natural persons, and it is natural persons whose interests should be our concern. I suggest that this loss has occurred, that as a result the outcome of events is only partly determined by the interests of natural persons, giving a society that functions less than fully in the interests of the persons who make it up. In addition to this objective suboptimum functioning, the loss of power brings about a widespread subjective feeling of powerlessness. Such a feeling appears to be quite general, occurring on both the left and the right, as well as among those persons at neither ideological extreme. A good example is provided by the following extended quotation.

Resign your responsibilities into the hands of the state or of some giant squid corporation, and it is their decisions, and not yours, that prevail. . . . Homes and workshops and the rooted communities into which they have naturally grouped by long processes of organic growth are now threatened as never before by an unholy alliance between all that is worst in capitalism and all that is worst in socialism or collectivism. . . . Local authorities, as greedy for rates as the tycoons are for profits, depopulate whole districts by compulsory purchase which instead of being a last desperate expedient in an exceptional crisis is abused as routine administrative blackmail.

Among the latest victims of these urban clearances are the craftsmen of Clerkenwell menaced by a project of the Islington Borough Council. . . .

Around the remains of the old priory of the Knights Hospitaliers beyond Smithfield Market there has grown up across the centuries a veritable colony of small individual craftsmen, clockmakers, wood carvers, jewellers, workers in metals, spinners, musical instrument makers, in clusters of little workshops hidden in the unpretentious old streets. . . .

These craftsmen are not representatives of dying trades. Their work is, if anything, more than even in demand but, on the one hand, they cannot pay the rents which oil companies, banks and insurance companies can pay, and, on the other, they are an untidy anomaly in the neat, inhuman calculations of the planners. . . . The fundamental and urgent issue is between the realities of human freedom and the dictatorial abstractions of the managerial state, between "us" and "them."[1]

If the power that has been lost by persons is to be recovered, if power is to be returned to natural persons, the first step is to examine those processes through which the loss takes place.

The Problem of Organization

When men join together to create a corporate actor, whether it is an industrial corporation, a trade union, a neighborhood association, or a political party, they find themselves

[1] Patrick Purpoole, "Comment," *The New Law Journal*, V, 122, Feb. 17, 1792, 164.

confronted with a dilemma: to gain the benefits of organization, they must give over the use of certain rights, resources,
or power to the corporate body. Only in this way can the
corporate actor have the necessary power to carry out the purposes for which they created it. But each person, in turning
over these rights, thereby loses a large measure of control
over them. For the corporate actor may well act in a direction
that he opposes. If, for example, three men join together in a
corporate body, and create a constitution that requires agreement from any two of them before it acts—a majority rule—
any one of them may find the corporate body acting against
his will. For the other two persons, there are four possible
patterns of preference toward any proposal: $++$, $+-$, $-+$,
and $--$. In two of these, the first and the last, the corporate
body will act or fail to act independently of his preference.
If he opposes the action but both others favor it, the corporate body will act. And if he favors it, but others oppose it,
the corporate body will not act. The point is obvious, but not
trivial: an individual, vesting certain resources in a corporate actor, no longer has full control over the use of those
resources.

There is one apparent remedy for this: to create a constitution such that the corporate resources can be committed
only when *all* corporators favor the action. This gives each
person a veto power over corporate action. The defect of this
solution, of course, is that the corporate actor is emasculated:
it can do nothing in the absence of unanimity of the members.
In the three-person case, only one pattern of eight is unanimous action; such a corporate body is prevented from acting in
seven of eight patterns. When the number of corporators of
the corporate actor is greater, say size N, there remains only
one pattern that is unanimity, while the number of non-
unanimous patterns is 2^N-1. Obviously, if N is large, the corporate actor will almost never act, unless there are special
conditions that bring about unanimity.

In society, we see different kinds of decision rules, more

or less restrictive, for different types of actions, and in different kinds of corporate bodies. A fire department's action may be triggered by a single individual's action in turning in an alarm. An action of a trade union or a corporation may take place when a majority of delegates or directors favors the action. A constitutional amendment in the United States requires a two-thirds majority in both houses of Congress, and a positive action by three fourths of the states. In the United Nations, an action of the Security Council requires unanimity among the five permanent members.

In business corporations in the United States, early charters from the states required a very restrictive decision rule to change the corporation's charter: unanimity among the owners. But such a restrictive rule obviously would make impossible the change of charter in a large corporation with very dispersed ownership. Soon the rules of incorporation were modified, so that votes of a subset of owners could change the charter, over the opposition of the others. This modification explicitly took power away from the owners as individuals, and placed it in the hands of the owners collectively, i.e., the corporate actor.[2]

Still another kind of decision rule is one which allows certain actions to be taken by a single agent of the corporate actor, a person who occupies the executive office or position. This, like the decision rule of a fire department, gives a high capacity for action to the corporate actor. Authority over a certain class of actions is delegated by the members or corporators to the executive officer, enabling him to act directly, without reference to their opinions.

These remarks point to the central dilemma of organization: by giving the corporate body power to act, each member largely loses his power over the direction its actions will take; but by withholding this power, through a more re-

[2] See Commons (1924) for an extended examination of this development.

strictive decision rule, the potential benefits brought by the corporate actor vanish.

This dilemma of organization holds not only in business corporations, in trade unions, and in other membership organizations; it holds for the state as well. That power which men hold corporately, through their government, they do not hold individually. One way, for example, of expressing the difference between liberal democracies and socialist democracies is the amount of power held individually by men (and by corporate actors independent on the state) relative to the amount they have vested in the single corporate actor, the state. In a socialist state, men hold much less of their power individually; much more is held by that special corporate actor, the state.

It is important to be clear about the sense in which natural persons, persons like you and me, have lost power to corporate actors through our investment of resources in those actors. The sense in which we do and do not have control over these resources can be described as follows, in different contexts:

1. If a person invests money in a corporation, he can sell his fraction of the capital assets at any time; or, if he can gain the assent of enough of his fellow investors, he can in fact unseat the corporation's directors.

But in the day-to-day operations of the corporation, the person as an investor has no control over the use of his capital. And in major corporate decisions, concerning new ventures, changes in management or directorships, declaration of dividends, and nearly any other use of the capital resources of which the corporation consists, he has no effective control unless he owns a sufficient fraction of the capital for his votes to make a difference.

2. If a worker joins a union, and thereby gives up to the union the rights of negotiating his wages and conditions of work, and gives it as well union dues, he may, if he can gain

the assent of enough others, come to have direct control of these rights through gaining control of the union's offices, or through voting to disband the union.

But in the day-to-day operations of the union, the member has no voice in the use of his vested rights by officers. The officers may engage a lobbyist for political goals he does not favor; they may agree to a wage settlement he opposes, or they may call a strike he does not want, or carry out a disciplinary action toward him, depriving him of certain union rights; or they may engage in a multitude of other activities, oblivious to his wishes, using the resources he has vested in them.

3. In a democratic state, a citizen, conceived to have a set of natural rights, gives up direct control over those rights to representatives, who in turn delegate those rights to government officials. The citizen retains control in the sense that he may, from time to time, recall his representatives if he can gain assent of enough other citizens. He may have other mechanisms, such as use of petition, impeachment, and recall, by which he can call back the use of his vested rights. And by gaining the assent of still more persons, he can dissolve and reconstitute this large corporate actor, the state.

But in the day-to-day operations of the government, the citizen has no voice in the use of his rights by government officials. They may use his taxes for purposes he abhors; they may pass laws which transfer some of his resources to others, laws which give or take away rights from individual persons and corporate actors; they may enter into agreements with other nation-states which alienate those rights still further from him.

In all of these cases, the individual person has given up to corporate actors not ultimate and absolute control over his rights, but effective and immediate control over these rights. In doing so, he undergoes a loss of control over his resources to corporate actors. In the area of property rights, this has been extensively described by Berle and Means in their study

of the modern corporation.[3] Showing the separation between
ultimate ownership of the capital of large corporations in the
U.S. and effective control of these assets, they conclude that
the traditional concept of private property has two com-
ponents: "passive property," or the rights of ownership, and
"active property," or the power-in-use of these economic resources. According to Berle and Means, the owners retain the
passive property rights, while the corporate managers hold
the active property rights, the power to use these assets. (My
earlier discussion, however, implies that not even the managers, as persons, hold the active property rights. They are
merely providing services to the corporate actor, acting as
trustees of those rights, and employing them in the interests
of the corporation.) A similar partitioning can be made for
other rights and resources as well: those of the worker who
is a union member, those of the citizen of a nation-state, those
of the member of any voluntary organization.

The first source of the loss of power from real persons to
corporate actors is that described above, the fact of organization itself. If a person vests some of his resources or some
of his sovereignty in a corporate actor, he does so under an
implicit contract with the corporate actor: the corporate actor
has use of these resources, to be employed for purposes that
the investors hope and expect will benefit them. Thus the
person makes the investment in the hope and expectation
that his loss of control over these resources will be more
than balanced by the greater benefits they will bring him
when combined with others.

This contract between the person, the source of power,
and the corporate actor, the user of power, is the constitution
of the corporate actor. The constitution describes the terms of
the contract, the specific rights and obligations of the persons and the corporate actor: the limitations on the corporate
actor in its use of the resources, and the conditions, including
voting rights and decision rules, under which the persons

[3] See Berle and Means (1940).

can exercise control over this use, by changing the officers or by giving explicit directives to the officers through a collective decision. And the constitution ordinarily includes another provision as well: the conditions under which the persons with ultimate rights can modify the constitution. Paradoxically, it is through use of this provision that persons in modern society have come to lose further power to corporate actors. Now we shall see how that occurs.

Changes in the Contract

There is both parallel interest and conflict of interest between the two sides to a constitutional contract, the persons (whom I will call "sovereigns" rather than "members," to explicitly signify that the resources ultimately reside in them) and the corporate actor. The parallel interests lie in the explicit purpose of the corporate actor, the purpose for which the sovereigns have combined their resources. The conflict of interest lies in the freedom of the corporate actor to use those resources. Full freedom, unshackled by the sovereigns, gives the greatest power to the corporate actor in its actions toward the outside environment; but this very lack of shackles further alienates the sovereigns from their resources.

Thus when the corporate actor comes into existence, a new set of interests comes into existence. This new set of interests consists primarily of interests toward freeing the corporate actor from the shackles imposed by the sovereigns. And in many areas, this set of interests, using the resources vested in it, has been successful in further alienating those resources from their source. The means by which this has taken place has been examined in some detail for two kinds of corporate actors: business corporations and trade unions.

Berle and Means (1940) discuss the evolution of the modern corporation, an evolution that has consisted largely in a further alienation of economic power by managers of corporations from owners. The alienation has taken place through a change in charter, that is, a change in the terms of contract between sovereigns and corporate actor. In the United States this has been particularly easy, because incorporation has been carried out by states, rather than the federal government, and states have competed to allow incorporation in terms attractive to the incorporators. These were ordinarily the original owner-managers, who, controlling the corporate actor, held as their own interests a maximum freedom of action for the corporate actor. Thus constitutions were created which paved the way toward a further alienation of power from the owners. In particular, these constitutions or charters allowed:

1. The use by management of proxy votes in the annual stockholders' meetings, so that by circulating stockholders, management could come to gain their votes for its proposals;

2. The possibility of changing the charter by majority vote of the stockholders, rather than requiring a larger fraction of the votes;

3. The possibility of issuance of stock (preferred stock, nonvoting common stock, stock in trust) which could bring in new capital from new partial owners without giving them voting rights;

4. The possibility that corporations themselves could hold voting stock in a corporation, thus paving the way for holding companies which, through a process of pyramiding, would allow owners of a tiny fraction of capital to control the corporation;[4]

4 Pyramiding is the stacking of holding companies on top of one another, with one or more operating companies at the bottom. Because the majority rule allows full control of a company by ownership of only 50+ percent of its voting stock, it is easy to calculate the number of stages necessary to control a corporate actor of a given size. Assume one man one vote for simplicity. Then we begin with two men who form a coalition, and start with a corporate actor of size 3. Then the successive corporate actors in which the preceding one would have a bare majority are 5, 9, 17, 33, 65 and so on. If there are m+1 stages, beginning with the 3-man collectivity, these two persons can exercise full control over a collectivity of size $2^m + 1$. With 11 stages, for example, two persons can control a collectivity of 1025 merely through the vagaries of the majority rule.

5. The freedom to locate annual stockholders' meetings at times and places that made it difficult for stockholders to attend;

6. The right to charge costs of obtaining stockholders' proxies as business costs, i.e., to subtract these costs from owners' profits.

Through these powers and others, the corporation was able to change the terms of its contract to satisfy its interests in freedom of action; and the stockholders increasingly lost control over the corporation. Some reversals occurred, when certain kinds of corporate actions were declared illegal by states, such as nonvoting common stock, or stock with voting rights disproportionate to its monetary value. But despite these laws, the general development continued, to the point where the interests of those persons who invest in a corporation are subordinated to the interests of the corporate actor itself. It is only through a stockholder revolt, the conditions for which have come to be very difficult, that the power of use of the sovereigns' capital can be revoked.

Trade unions show a similar development. The trade union constitution is a contract between the members and the union as a corporate actor designed to further their interests. The conditions of the contract can be restrictive or free for the corporate actor. But just as with business corporations, the power vested in that union, together with the new interests that came into being with formation of the union, has enabled it to modify the terms of the contract to increase its freedom of action and further alienate power from its source. Robert Michels (1949) recognized this some years ago in his study of the Social Democratic Party in Germany. The evolution of that party led him to state his famous "iron law of oligarchy": "It is organization which gives birth to the dominion of the elected over the electors, of the mandataries over the mandators, of the delegates over the delegators. Who says organization says oligarchy" (p. 401). Thus, in trade unions and workers' parties, just as with business corporations, power comes increasingly into the hands of the corporate body, and out of the hands of natural persons. The mechanisms through which this occurs, however, are somewhat different from those in business corporations. Some of them are:

1. Development and use of the cult of unity. The central fact about the trade union is that it has been through its history an adversary organization. An actor in a conflict needs great freedom of action to use its resources with greatest effect. This principle, and the membership interests it satisfies, has been used by many leaders of conflict organizations to reduce opposition. For example, the Communist Party of the Soviet Union introduced this resolution in their 1921 Congress:

All class-conscious workers must clearly realize the perniciousness and impermissibility of factionalism of any kind, for in practice factionalism inevitably results in weakening teamwork. At the same time it inevitably leads to intensified and repeated efforts by the enemies of the Party, who have fastened themselves onto it because it is the governing party to widen cleavage [in the party] and to use it for counterrevolutionary purposes.[5]

In trade unions a normative climate has developed against cleavage or opposition, a climate that has been termed, as indicated above, "the cult of unity." Many unions have clauses in their constitutions banning any suborganizations within the union designed to affect its direction. The effect of such a climate and such bans is to allow only *one* corporate actor, the union organization, and to fragment potential opposition. The end result is to reduce the possibility of organized opposition to incumbent leaders. This climate is sufficiently strong in many unions for it to be, as it is, used to justify the transfer of extraordinary powers to union officers.

2. A second mechanism to alienate power from its source in trade unions has been to change election procedures so that potential bases of organized opposition were powerless.

[5] See Lipset, Trow, and Coleman (1956), p. 271.

A single example will indicate the general principle.[6] After an initial factional fight in the Printing Pressmen's Union, the new president, George Berry, used his power to change rules for election of president. The new rules provided for an electoral-college system of election in which the largest locals had a maximum of six votes and the smallest locals had a minimum of one. The only organizational bases for opposition were in the large locals, like New York, and this reduction of their voting rights made that opposition ineffective. This constitutional change then allowed Berry to break a New York wildcat strike in 1919 by bringing in strikebreakers, without fear of powerful retribution from members of the New York local. Similarly, this power through constitutional change allowed him in the 1920s to expel locals which opposed him—and later allowed him to name his son as his successor. In short, the terms of the original contract between members and union gave Berry sufficient power to allow him to alienate further power from members by changing the contract itself.

3. There are many other aspects of the original contract that, by omission or intent, make possible the further alienation of power by the union from the members. Use of the membership list for appealing to members, and the right to withhold that list from others, gives the managers of the union a partial monopoly of information. Rights to use union funds to break down the potential for organization among members has a similar effect; and there are other available devices. The end effect has been as in the case of business corporations—an increasing separation of power from its source in persons, to be lodged in corporate actors.

The social structure that these processes have brought about is a social structure in which a large fraction of the important transactions in society—those transactions important to persons—are carried out by powerful corporate actors over which persons have little or no control. Persons receive

[6] *Ibid.*, p. 445.

benefits from those corporate actors, ordinarily sufficient to prevent a membership or owner revolt. But these corporate actors are, in their actions, motivated toward purposes of their own—very often purely growth—for which membership benefits are viewed merely as a constraint. For example, some economists now conceive of the rate of return to capital—the owner's benefits—as merely one of the constraints, like wages, that those agents who control a corporation must take into account, rather than as a corporate goal.

In this circumstance, it is not unreasonable for ordinary persons to see themselves as mere pawns in a game that is played by other actors. Yet it is difficult for persons to see just who these actors are. They are not the managers of corporations, unions, associations, for these managers are mere persons themselves, whose services are used by the corporate actors. It is the corporate actors, the organizations that draw their power from persons and employ that power to corporate ends, that are the primary actors in the social structure of modern society.

What does this mean, in practice? It means a peculiar bias in the direction that social and economic activities take. It means that among the variety of interests that men have, those interests that have been successfully collected to create corporate actors are the interests that dominate the society. It is not so simple as persons' interests vs. corporate actors' interests, because each corporate actor acts to satisfy certain of these interests. But this state of affairs means that decisions about the employment of resources are more and more removed from the multiplicity of dampening and modifying interests of which a real person is composed—more and more the resultant of a balance of narrow intense interests of which corporate actors are composed.[7] Thus, to simplify an

[7] Sasha Weitman (1972) shows this in the case of nations, showing that they are simpler, more primitive actors than are persons. Their primitive character is not something intrinsic to social organization per se, compared to psychic organization, but is the result of the specific forms of social organization that men have invented—just as

example, the highway taxes on trucking will be the outcome of the balance of interests among the trucking industry and the Teamsters Union on the one hand, and the railway industry and the railway unions on the other. Interests of natural persons who are not incorporated, not part of the conflicts and bargains among corporate actors, will not enter.

It means also that as men's interests change, the change is less and less easily reflected in the important activities of society, because the interests are cast into corporate structure, and the actions are insulated from the men who gave the corporate actors their power.

This structure of society means that those persons whose resources have not been combined together to form corporate actors find themselves especially helpless. For them, it is not only some of their interests which fail to be represented in the corporate actions of which society is made up; it is all their interests that are left out of the balance.[8]

The Psychic Consequences

There is one further matter of some importance. The preceding discussion implies that there has been in the past half-century a great loss of power from persons to corporate actors. As I have indicated, this occurs in part through the mere increase in size of corporate actors in which one has made an investment—and then it occurs in part because this very transfer of power from sovereign persons to a central locus in a corporate actor places in the hands of the corporate actor the weapons by which a further alienation of power can take place.

But there is another process that must increasingly give

---

the medieval corporate body is more primitive than the modern bureaucratic corporate actor.

[8] These persons are those whom a number of authors have discussed under the concept of "mass society." See Lipset, Trow, and Coleman (1956, Chap. 2) and Kornhauser (1959).

persons a sense of loss of control over matters that concern them. Through the enormous transformation of the structure of communication in society, persons are concerned about matters extending to a much wider horizon than was once the case. Events that were unknown or unimportant to them are now brought vividly to their attention and thereby made important. Even if the structure of control of events by corporate actors—nations, corporations, labor unions, and others —had not changed at all, those faraway events that are under the control of very large corporate actors are much more readily and fully communicated to persons than they were even before the advent of television.

For these reasons, including both the objective drift of power from persons to ever-larger corporate actors and the increasing attention to those events controlled by very large corporate actors (often events in which nations are the actors), the subjective experience of persons should include a greater sense of powerlessness than was true, say, fifty years ago.

One sees this sense of powerlessness in a variety of everyday activities. An interesting recent development in many cities brings to light for newspaper readers some of the frustrations that bring this sense of powerlessness. A number of newspapers have initiated a service in which readers call or write about problems; the newspaper attempts to solve them, and then publishes the problems and their solutions in a special column. In one of these columns, "Direct Line" in the Baltimore *Evening Sun*, a count of items over a ten-day period showed a large majority of the items to be problems expressed by natural persons in their capacity as natural persons (not as agents of corporate actors), in their transactions with corporate actors of two kinds: business firms and governmental agencies. The following item from January 3, 1972 presents a case in which both types of corporate actors were involved:

"I'm in some sort of a bind over a contract I signed, upon my return from duty in Vietnam, with a recognized correspondence school.

"I was to pay $15 per month and the Veterans Administration was to reimburse me. For six months I didn't get a single work assignment from the school although I'd made the payments.

"Pressing my inquiries on what happened, I learned all my papers had been lost and the whole procedure would have to be reprocessed.

"Nevertheless, the school's credit bureau is threatening court action unless I pay the full amount due under the contract. I can't do this until I get the money from the VA. Can you help straighten out this mess for me, please?—R.M.B."

"A review of the records indicates that certification of lessons completed for the period October 1, to December 21, had not been made by either the veteran or the school," J. E. Mueller, contact officer for the VA, wrote Direct Line.

"A card has been sent the veteran and when this has been filled in and returned, the VA will initiate action to reimburse the veteran for lessons completed for the above period," he wrote.

Although one can conjecture that the sense of powerlessness has increased over time as persons' interactions with large corporate actors has increased, it is only in the past ten years that sociologists have begun to measure persons' feelings of power or powerlessness vis-à-vis the environment. Julian Rotter developed a measure which he describes as internal control (that is, a sense of control by oneself of the activities that affect him) vs. external control (the sense of being subject to control by forces outside oneself). Melvin Seeman has extensively used a similar measure, which he calls a measure of powerlessness. The only examination over time with similar populations using such a measure is a pair of studies by Rotter, in which he administered the same measure to a sample of college student populations in 1962 and a comparable sample in 1971. Rotter (1971) found a large decline in the feeling of internal control between 1962 and 1971, or as Seeman would describe it, an increase in the sense of powerlessness.

Such a short-term variation is very likely due to short-term fluctuations in events rather than a long-term secular trend. But it does show that there are sharp differences at different times in persons' sense of powerlessness.

This fact, coupled with the objective loss of power from persons to corporate actors, would not be important if a sense of powerlessness were itself an unimportant element of a person's psychic life. But Seeman (1963, 1967) and others have shown that it is a very important element. By several ingenious experiments, he has shown that persons who feel powerless do not *learn* as much about their environment as those who believe they have power to control events. He has shown that persons with a sense of powerlessness show *lack of interest* in international affairs (1966) and a *lack of political knowledge* (1971 a, b) and Ransford (1968) has shown that students with a sense of powerlessness are more likely to engage in violence, in outbreaks of protest like the Free Speech Movement in Berkeley.[9,10]

It is clear from all this work that the subjective sense of control that persons feel is very important to their psychological well-being. It has not been shown that the loss of power from persons to corporate actors generates a sense of loss of control or powerlessness; but if it does so, then the processes I have described here, processes that have taken place largely in this century, have imposed very widespread psychic costs on persons throughout modern society.

But recognizing all this provides a start toward remedying it. We may ask the question, What can be done to bring about

[9] Seeman quotes Seale and McConville's (1968, p. 226) description of the motives of the French intellectuals who joined the May protest: "It was a revolt against ruling bureaucracies, administrative machines, professional apparatuses. It found expression in an urge to run one's own affairs." These imputed motives are the direct subjective counterpart of the objective loss of power to corporate actors that I have described here.

[10] Seeman compared, in some of these same studies, measures of the classical Marxist concept of alienation from work—which is argued by Marxists to have debilitating psychological and social effects. He found that the alienation from work which was its supposed psychologi-

restitution, to restore power to its source in natural persons? It is a beginning toward an answer to this question to which the third chapter is directed.

---

cal effect—that is, the "meaningfulness" of one's work, the "intrinsic satisfactions" from the work—showed little relation to psychic malaise, while one's sense of lack of control of those events of interest to him showed a very strong relation to such psychic distress.

3

RESTITUTION

It is useful to conceive of two stages in the history of modern corporate actors. The first was the stage in which they replaced the fixed estates of feudal society, and constituted a vehicle for the enlargement of men's newly won freedom—a vehicle for bringing to realization the "natural rights" of which seventeenth-century philosophers wrote. In this first stage, the corporate actor is, to be sure, a new element in social structure—a juristic person come to take its place alongside natural persons as an element in the social structure. But in its early days, the corporate actor was never very far from man's control—although that control was often very unequally distributed among men. The second stage in the history of corporate actors has come only in the twentieth century, a stage in which many corporate actors have come to be largely autonomous, largely out from under the control of men. It is like the recurrent science-fiction nightmare—the robot created by man coming to have a will of its own, and out from under the control of man. The fact that these robots are merely intangible organizational structures makes them no less real in their effects. Their single-minded pursuit of narrow interests is softened by the fact that they employ human beings to fill their positions and carry out their goals, and these human beings are not so single-purposed. Nevertheless, it is persons who are working for the corporate actors, and not the reverse. For these corporate actors, the wants and interests of persons (whether those persons are owners of capital assets, members, employees, customers, clients, or whatever) constitute only constraints on a path of which the goal is corporate survival and growth.

In such a situation, society has come to be inhabited, in

the twentieth century, with a new set of powerful purposive actors. It is our task to examine how these corporate actors can be made subservient to natural persons. In this chapter, I will attempt to describe some of the devices by which this may be done—as well as to provide some warnings against other devices which carry danger in their consequences.

It is necessary first to look more closely at some of the specific means by which certain types of corporate actors exercise power. Only then will it be possible to see how restitution might take place.

First, considering business corporations, one may ask the question whether restitution to the *owners or members* of a corporate actor is in fact appropriate. Berle and Means raise this question at the end of their examinations of the separation of ownership and control in modern corporations. Their answer is No—that given the alienation of control from ownership, it is appropriate that the control be used not to implement the interests of owners, not to implement the personal interests of managers, and not to implement the growth-and-survival interests of the corporations as actors. Rather, they suggest, the expropriated power should be put to use in the interests of the "community as a whole." Their argument, however, is weak; their discussion both vague and naïve. Some means by which this might occur have been recently proposed, in particular election of public interest members to corporation boards of directors. Yet even if public interest members were on boards of directors, either by fiat or by some fad among owners leading to election of such members, it is not clear just what interests they would pursue, and whether the result would any better reflect persons' interests.[1]

---

[1] The boards of trustees of nonprofit corporations, like foundations, present an interesting case: Is their commission to act in the "public interest" or in the foundation's interest? Managers of government agencies are intended to be "public servants," acting in the "public interest." But the vagaries of their actions, and the degree to which those actions reflect the interests of the government as corporate actor, indicate that the "public interest" is not necessarily pursued by persons who purport to act in its behalf.

Furthermore, there is no theoretical rationale for the legiti-
macy of such a transfer of rights or redistribution of resources.

On the other hand, F. A. v. Hayek (1960) argues that the
rights and resources held by those in control of corporations
should go back to owners. He specifies two mechanisms by
which such restitution could occur. First, owners, not managers, should have the right individually to determine allocation of the net product of their capital. Dividend rates
should be based on the total increment in the corporation's
assets, leaving the individual owners, rather than the managers, to decide how much to reinvest and how much to withdraw for consumption or investment elsewhere. He suggests
also that in voting by owners, only individual owners of stock,
and not corporations as owners, be allowed to vote. The first
mechanism is designed to reduce imperfections in the capital
market, by putting the reinvestment decision in the hands of
those—the stockholders—whose interest is to realize the greatest return on their capital, rather than those—the managers—
whose interest is primarily in growth of the particular firm.
The second is designed to prevent use of the majority decision rule to concentrate control in the hands of a small minority of owners, through pyramiding.

The first mechanism, however, appears hardly necessary,
because the fluctuation in stock prices, and the highly effi-
cient capital market, restores to owners a portion of their
control—simply because that market forces corporations to
cater to the interests of owners.

Thus despite the apparent concentration of power in the
hands of these corporate actors, it would appear that the
capital market itself restores a large measure of power to
owners, by forcing corporations to attend to the interests of
owners and potential owners in order to attract capital.

Does this then mean that the apparent drift of power from
owners to corporate actors is illusory, and that the corporate
actors have little power despite their independence from
owners' votes? I think not. For we must look at this corporate

actor in all the markets in which it operates, and then ask for each whether there is a power asymmetry that allows it to extract a larger share of value from the transaction. If we look at the business corporation in this way, it appears as a mechanism which partitions up the value added by its production among persons in the different markets in which it engages. Suppose a business corporation operates in four markets: a capital market, a raw materials market, a labor market, and a product market. If the corporation is small relative to all corporations in the capital market, as nearly all are, then it cannot extract extra value from this market. But if it is large relative to the product market, as is the case when there are few firms in an industry, and if the buyers are large in number and thus small in size, then there is an imbalance of power. This imbalance will allow it to extract excess value from the consumers.

The power has traditionally been seen to consist primarily in the possibility of oligopolistic practices, such as price-fixing. But this is probably a naïve view, arising from the well-developed character of price theory in economics. What appears to be more nearly true is that it is the size or power disparity itself between producer and consumer that creates the possibility of extracting greater value from the transaction. For this disparity determines who controls the conditions surrounding the transaction, particularly *information* relevant to the transaction.[2] Information, in the form of market research and advertising, can bring about the conditions of a partial monopoly, by creating a taste for the particular corporation's product, i.e., the particular brand. Once such a partial monopoly is established and maintained, the corporate actor can thereby extract greater value from the transaction. Similarly, the size and thus power of the corporation means that it can hire salesmen; but the consumer cannot hire buyers. Thus, sophistication and knowledge about the

[2] I am indebted to Z. A. Walaszek for focusing my attention on problems of information in social transactions.

transaction lie much more in the hands of the corporate actor than the person. If, in markets where natural persons are consumers and corporations the producers, we compare the expenditures on market research, advertising, and salesmen —all designed to further the interests of the corporate actor— with those on consumer research, publication of consumer information, and buyers, designed to further the interest of the consumer, something of the magnitude of this imbalance in dictating the conditions of the transaction can be seen. This imbalance contrasts greatly with the relative balance between expenditures in intermediate markets by buyer and seller, both corporate actors of similar size. First, advertising expenditures are much less than in consumer markets; and second, there exist buyers, and there exists work devoted to laying out specifications, and work devoted to evaluation of competitive bids or testing of competitive products.

If there is a power asymmetry in certain of a corporate actor's markets and not in others, the corporation appears as a *biased* mechanism for partitioning the value it adds among persons in different markets. In particular, if it has greater power than the consumer in its product markets, so that these markets are not close to being highly competitive, but its capital markets and materials markets are highly competitive, and its labor markets are subject to tight bargaining, then this should produce a partitioning of the value created by the corporation in which the consumer gets little (i.e., prices are monopolistic, or goods are of low quality relative to price), and the owner and worker get much. Insofar as this is true the corporation can thereby be seen as a device for producing a general flow of value from consumer to owner and worker and supplier.[3] It may be this process, operating

---

[3] Most authors, insofar as they raise the question of power in productive firms rather than assuming perfect markets and using the theory of marginal products, consider only the relative power of the factors of production, i.e., capital and labor, examining the types of markets— and relative power in the market—in which capital and labor are bought by the firm. E. Preiser (1952) also looks at differences in elasticity of

over a period of years, that produces the curious paradox of increasing incomes and increasing wealth, on the one hand, and an increasingly shoddy set of things on which to spend that wealth. The desire to buy cheaply, throw away, and buy again, is not an intrinsic one, nor is such a pattern as fully in the interests of consumers as of producers. The desire is clearly one that has been built up over a period of years in consumers by producers through their control of information surrounding the transaction. This is not, of course, to say that all changes in products that are decried by some consumers have been more in the producer's interest than the consumer's. To argue that would be to hold to a romantic traditionalism. Prepared food, for example, in contrast to unprocessed meat, vegetables, fruit, and grain, has probably developed to meet changing interests of consumers rather than interests of producers. The decline in women's cooking and housekeeping activities has created a strong demand for highly processed prepared food that requires almost no home preparation.

Altogether, without yet specifying how the process of restitution might take place, we can say that restitution in the case of a business corporation is not merely a matter of returning power from managers back to its original locus in the hands of owners. It involves, rather, an examination of where a corporation can use its power in such a way that it can extract disproportionate value from the transaction. Though the corporation *obtained* its power from its investors, its ability to *use* this power depends upon the relative strength—through the market, as in the capital market, or through organizations, as with trade unions—of those with whom it engages in transactions.

Matters are somewhat different for corporate actors in the form of labor unions. There is nothing comparable for a worker in a plant to a capital market for an investor. Thus a

demand for and supply of labor in driving its price below the marginal product. But the existence of labor unions with large treasuries has reduced sharply the inelasticity of labor supply.

worker often does not have the effective alternative of exercising power by leaving the union, as an investor does by selling his stock. The power disparity *is* a power disparity between the corporate actor, the union, and its members, the workers. Restitution in this case involves first an examination of just how the corporate actor exercises its power vis-à-vis the members. In contrast to business corporations in relation to their owners, unions exercise their power over members primarily through authoritative actions which the members must obey: disciplinary actions, agreement to collective bargaining settlements, obedience to union rules, acceptance of taxes. The situation is much like that in a political democracy, where the primary means of redress against the corporate actor is exercising control over it, through elections or other collective actions.[4]

Doing this requires, as research on trade unions has shown, *organization*, to provide potential alternatives to those who currently govern the union.[5] If organization is costly and difficult, as it is in most trade unions, then the corporate actor holds a great deal of power over the members. If organization is easy, as in a few trade unions, then the corporate actor has not alienated power from members.[6] What it has done is to concentrate that power for use against

[4] See A. O. Hirschman (1971) for an examination of the two major means by which persons can exercise control vis-à-vis the corporate actor: "exit" and "voice."

[5] See Lipset, Trow, and Coleman (1956).

[6] The existence of membership strength vis-à-vis the union as a corporate actor does not imply that the union will behave in ways seen as more "responsible" by other parties. In fact, the opposite may be true, as the closer control by members leads to harder bargaining on the part of leaders. For example, the International Typographical Union, perhaps the North American union in which most power resides in the members, has engaged in a series of strikes and wage negotiations that has forced a number of newspapers out of business, and in some cities threatens to make newspapers themselves uneconomic. This is very likely a rational action on the part of union members, whose interest is more nearly in present wages and job conditions than in future jobs, since they are relatively old. (In 1952, the average age of New York members of the ITU was over 45; since then, it has probably increased.)

others, while the members themselves are protected by the internal organizational devices they have constructed.

Such organization implies either the construction of ad hoc temporary corporate actors, or the use of existing corporate actors that are composed of union members, but not subordinate to the union as a whole. In the International Typographical Union, for example, there have been continuing organizations in the form of various benefit associations, monotype and linotype clubs (which serve as employment agencies for monotypists and linotypists), and the large locals themselves. These corporate actors, though designed for other purposes, can provide the power base for opposition to those who control the union's offices, at election time and to a lesser extent between elections. They have independent channels of information to the members, and men whose time is available for work opposing the leaders.

The general proposition, covering both labor unions and business corporations, can be put in this way: When there has been alienation of power by a corporate actor from its source in persons, then there is no necessity for restitution back to that source if there is a highly competitive market, allowing easy entry to and withdrawal of persons from the corporate actor. In that case, restitution is provided by the power of the market, against which the power of the corporate actor is small. Then, however, it is necessary to look for the corporate actor's use of that power it has received against persons *other than* the original sovereigns. In the case of business corporations, that might be workers, it might be suppliers, it might be customers. If there is *not* easy and nearly costless entry to and withdrawal from the corporate actor, as in labor unions, then restitution of power back to the sovereigns is necessary. This appears to be possible principally through the construction of countervailing corporate actors which can act as coalitions within the larger corporate actors. These may exist in the form of independent organizations with many of the same members as the larger corporate actor, or opposition political parties. If they do not exist, then the possibility of restitution appears to lie in nearly costless means of creating such organization, i.e., competing corporate actors.

The two types of corporate actors I have examined in the discussion to this point are business corporations and labor unions. It would hardly be possible to examine here all types of corporate actors which have alienated power from sovereign persons. However, it is useful to consider some different examples of corporate actors in their transactions with persons, to examine the nature of power disparities between them and persons, and possibly to provide some insight into the means by which persons could gain greater power in these transactions.

An interesting and relatively benign first example which I know in some detail concerns admission to higher education.[7] In the admissions process, there is a very large and complicated matching process necessary between applicants and universities. Information is necessary for both parties, in order for each to act to implement his interests. Applicants want information about universities; universities want information about applicants, to decide whom they would like to have as students. The current state of affairs is this: Applicants must provide universities with directly comparable information prescribed by the universities, largely in the form of test scores from the College Entrance Examination Board or the American College Testing program. Universities and colleges provide information that is *not* comparable, determined by *them*, in the form of their college catalogs. The result is that universities and colleges are much better able to realize *their* interests—which overlap with those of applicants, but are not identical to them—than students are able to realize theirs.

How did this come about? Agents of universities and colleges, with concentrated power, met and created a corporate

7 I have discussed this in more detail in Coleman (1969).

actor—the CEEB—and as an oligopoly, dictated terms of admission to applicants, whose resources were dispersed: each applicant to one of the "member" universities would have to submit scores on a test, the costs of which he paid.[8]

No such agency has developed to implement the interests of applicants. Applicants do not know rates of admission of a university's graduates to professional schools, graduate schools, or firms of particular characteristics. They do not know the amount of time that faculty members spend with students outside class. They do not know departments' Cartter ratings, how graduates or current students at a university rate or describe it on a variety of dimensions. They do not know dropout rates, proportions of students in various fields, or a variety of other measures that would benefit them in their choice. Furthermore, universities and colleges are quite resistant to providing such systematic and comparable data on themselves.[9] Without the concentrated power held by universities and colleges, applicants could not create their agent, a counterpart to the CEEB, to engage in consumer research on universities; and without the oligopoly held by universities, they cannot dictate that specific items of information be provided for them. Universities, consequently, have not been subject to the same market discipline as have students; and the character of universities has less fully evolved to meet the needs and interests of students than would be true if power in the college admissions market had been equally

[8] It is not my intention here to argue that the existence of CEEB testing has not been beneficial to students. I believe it has, for example, served a very important democratizing function in college admissions, as well as creating incentives among applicants toward scholastic achievement as the primary criterion for university admission. I want here to show only the asymmetry of benefits in this relation between corporate actors and persons. The lack of systematic information on colleges, for example, has meant lack of a comparable incentive for universities to improve in those things most important to applicants.

[9] On a voluntary basis, and under prodding from their agent, CEEB, some institutions have provided average SAT test scores for their entering student bodies. And some information is available from commercial sources. But the amount is very small, and very poorly financed, compared to the information provided for colleges.

distributed between persons and corporate actors. If that power had been equal, so that the applicants could obtain accurate information about the teaching of faculty and the faculty-student interaction, there could never have developed among faculty the disregard for teaching and for the interests of students that has characterized universities where faculty engage in research. The imbalance of activities and rewards in universities that leads to neglect of students would have quickly become apparent in information about the universities, and thus have been used by students as a basis for choices which would constitute pressure upon the university for change.

In this admissions example, the structural problem between corporate actor and person is the same as the structural problem between business corporations and persons in consumer markets. In both cases, the excess power of the corporate actor allows it to dictate the terms of the transaction to suit its interests, and only incidentally some of the interests of persons, with neglect of others of those interests. Restitution of power to persons in this case can well take the form of establishing power symmetry in the transaction.

Another example of the power of corporate actors and individual actors involves public school systems, which constitute subordinate corporate actors to the state.

An extended illustration will show some of the problems in controlling this corporate actor, together with some of the mechanisms by which such control may be exercised. Schools constitute an especially interesting case, because in the United States, one of the explicit functions of the public school has been seen to be that of the "melting pot": a melting pot for different immigrant groups, but also among social classes, and different racial and ethnic groups. From the beginning of public schools in this country, there was a single "common school," in contrast to the class-differentiated educational systems of Europe. Thus, schools have been, throughout U.S. history, a means of gaining both individual and collective ends: individual ends of education and skills, collective ends of helping to create a single society from a multiplicity of cultures and class backgrounds. Education, then, quite apart from constituting an individual right to be provided by local government to all persons independently of their ability to pay, is also in part a collective good.

The organization of schools in any large metropolitan area exhibits several problems having to do with large corporate actors. Affluent residents of a city leave the large city system for a smaller suburban system, in part because they cannot exercise control of their schools directly, and thus withdraw their resources and reinvest them in a school district they prefer.[10] This flight from the city creates a maldistribution of educational resources and thwarts the collective goals of education that the "common school" aimed to implement. These problems, together with others caused by problems of managing lower-class schools in the city and increasing costs of doing so, reduce further the ability of city schools to carry out their task.

The interests in education that appear not to be well met by the organization that has evolved appear to be principally three: first, among those whose educational background is poor, an increase in educational opportunity to equal that of children from more advantaged backgrounds (an interest not directly opposed by the latter); second, greater control over the conditions and characteristics of one's child's education, an interest held by persons at all economic levels; and third, the collective interest in helping to create a single society from disparate cultures. In some of these areas, there are obviously simply conflicts between different persons' interests, which would exist however schools were organized, that is, despite the form of the corporate actor. But others are interests which, though held in common, are not imple-

[10] In part, of course, the reason is purely economic. By moving to a district in which local taxes need not be distributed to the poor, who provide little tax money, they get greater expenditures on their child per tax dollar they spend.

mented by the corporate actors as currently constituted. The interests of the corporate actors as actors, as evidenced in the actions of school administrators, have been primarily to maintain organizational order and equilibrium. But the interests of persons who are served by the school (in some cases amplified through the use of corporate actors outside the schools, such as civil rights groups) have led to proposals or actions of the sorts described below.

1. Through the Congress persons have allocated tax funds to supplement educational expenditures for disadvantaged children. The principal instrument has been Title I of the Elementary and Secondary Education Act. Evaluation of these expenditures have indicated primarily one thing: they were used to implement the interests of the corporate actor, the school system, or its agents, in ways that implemented few interests of the persons they were designed to aid. For example, they were more often used to pay teachers for summer training than to pay for additional contact hours between teacher and children, or for that matter, *any* additional activities of the children themselves. They were seldom used in a way that any unbiased observer would expect to best implement the interests of the disadvantaged children.

2. Class actions have been brought in court by families of some children to require the school system to institute affirmative integration of the schools, in some cases including bussing. This has been opposed by the school systems primarily on the basis of maintaining organizational order, by arguments that it is unfeasible. When successful, implementation of the court order has often led to opposition from other persons also served by the school, who were not among the plaintiffs in the class action. (This action does not show conflicts of interest between persons and corporate actors, but between persons.)

3. There have been proposals to change the structure of control: for the large corporate actor, the city school system, to delegate its authority to new corporate actors, created for

the purpose in local areas of the city, giving "community control." This, where it has occurred, has implemented one interest of persons, the interest in greater control over their childrens' education, but at the expense of the other two: by creating homogeneous districts, the inequality of resources is increased, and the collective interest in creating a single society is made more difficult. In addition, the increase in a person's control through a reduction in school district size from 1,000,000 to 30,000 as in New York City may not be very great. According to one means of calculating, it is an increase from about 3 one-hundred thousandths to 2.5 one thousandths.[11] Both are very very small.

4. Class action suits on behalf of particular persons have been brought against a corporate actor, the state, on the basis of inequality of expenditures among different districts. Successful class actions have been carried out in several states. The most direct way of implementing the successful suits is for the state to remove control from the subordinate corporate actors, the local districts, and administer the schools of the state with state tax funds through a larger corporate actor, the state department of education. This would slightly implement one interest of low-income persons, that of equalizing educational opportunity (though only slightly, since in many metropolitan areas, educational expenditures on central-city low-income students are greater than those on higher-income suburban students, and since increases in effective educational opportunity depend on the mix of children in the school, and not merely on the level of school financing). But it would do so at the expense of the interest in local control of schools through smaller administrative districts.

5. There have been proposals to drastically change the power of the corporate actor through introduction of an explicit market system, with vouchers in the hands of par-

[11] See Coleman (1971).

ents. The corporate actors, public and private schools, would be subject to the discipline of a market, thus losing power to persons, as families of all income levels could move their children from one school to another. The transfer of power from the school system to families, i.e., from corporate actors to persons, lies in altering the flow of money: from persons in taxes to the state, followed by direct redistribution to persons, and from them to the schools, in exchange for services. This would replace a flow from persons to the state, then to the subordinate corporate actors, the school districts, and finally in the form of services, to the persons. To illustrate geographically, the current flow is: Persons $\xrightarrow{\text{(money)}}$ State $\xrightarrow{\text{(money)}}$ Schools $\xrightarrow{\text{(services)}}$ Persons. The proposed flow is: Persons $\xrightarrow{\text{(money)}}$ State $\xrightarrow{\text{(money)}}$ Persons $\underset{\text{(money)}}{\overset{\text{(services)}}{\rightleftarrows}}$ Schools.

This would implement fully persons' interest in control over their children's education, and would partially implement the interest of equalizing educational opportunity. It would do so at the expense of the collective socializing goal, because such individual choice would likely lead to social homogeneity of schools. In addition, it is clear that the near-monopoly of information over its performance in specific tasks (teaching reading and arithmetic) that a school presently maintains would prevent persons from effectively implementing their interests.

But one proposal modifying such a market system is especially interesting in its implications for the power of corporate actors and persons. This is for the state to place two additional constraints on the corporate actors to deal with the two above problems: first, removal of full rights of acceptance and rejection of students, by establishing upper and lower bounds for the proportion of different racial or socioeconomic groups in the school; and second, a requirement for measurement and full disclosure of performance information that is of interest to parents and children. These two constraints are interesting in that they accomplish the collective goals by removing rights, not from persons, but from the corporate actors, the schools.

This illustration shows various kinds of modification of corporate structure that might be designed to increase the realization of interests of persons. They range from using the existing corporate structure to attempt to modify the distribution of services to persons all the way to bypassing completely the corporate structure and placing resources directly in the hands of persons, with which they then create a market to control the corporate actors. The example is complicated by the fact that some of the interests that these changes are designed to implement are in conflict. But it does show one thing, through the last proposed change: that the existence of collective goals (making educational opportunity independent of income, and creating a single society through a common school) does not require the creation of ever larger and more powerful corporate actors. Here persons have *individual* interests and *collective* interests in education. They can implement their individual interests when they have resources to allocate, as with vouchers; they can realize their collective interests first by voting to tax and redistribute, and second, by imposing, through the state, constraints upon the corporate actors, in this case, the schools which accept the vouchers. Such a mechanism would constitute, in the ever-present struggle for power between corporate actors and natural persons, an increase in the power of natural persons.

Three Paths to Control of Corporate Actors

There are three paths to the control of corporate actors, and it is most important to distinguish between them. One is a path which uses new options of choice to bring the control of corporate actors back to individual persons—not necessarily those persons who are its "members" or its "owners," but possibly others. A simple example of such a device (how effective it might be is not relevant to the present point) is the voucher system in education described earlier. Another is the creation of capital markets with prices for stocks, which allowed owners of business corporations to regain some of the power inherent in their capital.

A second path toward control of corporate actors is the use of "fire to fight fire," the creation of countervailing corporate actors to offset the power of existing ones. Trade unions offer an example of a countervailing organization which has, for workers, gained the size and power necessary to press their interests against the actions of the employing corporation. The very example, however, suggests some of the limitations of this path of countervailing corporate actors.

The third path toward control of corporate actors is their subordination through the ultimate power, the state. One example is nationalization of industry; another is the operation of all major social institutions under state control, as in socialism.[12]

The third of these alternative paths to restitution, control by the state, derives from a different conception of sovereignty than do the first two. The difference between these conceptions may be expressed by a pair of terms coined by Walter Ullman (1966), the "descending theory" and the "ascending theory" of government. In the Middle Ages, the former theory saw sovereignty located in the state or in the king, and thus the government as a vast set of offices with concessions of power from the king. This political theory was supported by formal law, in which power resided ultimately in the king or the pope. The latter theory conceived of sovereignty as residing in the individual, gave rise to borough and town self-government, derived from common law, and in the Middle Ages had its philosophical justification from the contractual basis of the vassal-lord relationship.

[12] See Charles Reich (1966). Reich examines the principles that can develop in law to protect persons' interests as property rights are eroded in a welfare state.

With the advent of the natural rights philosophers in the seventeenth century, a parallel set of conceptions of sovereignty arose, though these developed a greater degree of complexity. The one, expressed by Hobbes and Locke, paralleled the ascending theory of government, in that it located natural rights in persons *individually*, some of them alienable, like ownership of private property, and others inalienable, like the rights of freedom of worship and freedom of speech. Government, in this theory, is a relatively passive instrument whose principal function is to protect these rights, both inalienable rights like freedom of speech and alienable rights like ownership of private property. Free corporate actors are consistent with this theory, for they consist merely of the joining together by some persons of their rights and resources to gain strength through combination. The principal argument against this theory, as expressed best, perhaps, by C. B. McPherson (1962), has been that the very alienability of certain of these rights, inherent in the concept of private property, has created the possibility for serious inequalities of rights and resources among different persons.[13] What has not been recognized in either the theory or in criticism of it is that the very combination of resources possible under this theory can create a set of powerful corporate actors in society which have a set of distinct interests that differ from those of the persons who created them.

The second conception of natural rights of sovereignty, initiated by Rousseau and culminating in Marx, parallels in some respects the "descending theory of government." In this theory, natural rights inhere in men *collectively*. The implication of this is that such alienable rights as private property do not exist, because they imply individual holdings. Government, in this theory, is the single collective in-

[13] John Rawls, in a series of papers culminating in a book (1971), has provided the first major extension of utilitarian theory to incorporate ideas of equality along with the original ideas of freedom inherent in it.

strument of persons' wills, with its principal function to implement these wills. Corporate actors, subordinate to the state, come into existence as instruments of the state, and thus indirectly of people's will. The principal argument against this theory has been that such rights held collectively are separated or alienated from persons, and instead are held by their users, that is, by the managers of the single large corporate actor, the state. Thus, in the absence of rights held individually, especially property rights, it is not possible to combine resources to form corporate actors, and thus not possible to concentrate sufficient power to provide a check or constraint on the use of power held by the state's managers. What has not been recognized by either the theorists or their critics is that the subordinate corporate bodies, set up as instruments of the state, come to have interests of their own. With their delegated resources, they implement those interests, interests that are sometimes antagonistic to the purposes of the state. Furthermore, those special interests of subordinate corporate actors may gain in power by the absence of the power of a competitive market.

This third path, the subordination of all corporate actors under control of one corporate actor, the state, can probably be viable only if the state itself has not aliented power from its citizens, and they have the power to oppose it when necessary. But as the earlier analysis indicated, persons can have power vis-à-vis a corporate actor in which they have investments only when they are free to withdraw without cost, or have the organized power through other corporate actors to exercise countervailing power. The first condition does not hold for citizens; and when all the corporate actors within the state are subordinate to the state, the second condition does not hold either. (That is, it does not hold except for the point mentioned earlier: that subordinate corporate actors come to have both interests and power of their own, thus possibly serving as the base for organized opposition to the state.) To some degree, then, control by persons of a state in which all corporate actors are subordinate is a contradiction in terms.[14]

Because of these inherent problems in this third path toward control by persons—subordination to the state—I will consider only the first two paths. This does not mean, however, that the state cannot be used in a different way: to modify the distribution of rights between corporate actors and persons, by removing some of the rights of corporate actors, or increasing those of persons. It is useful to indicate how that might occur.

A Note on the Law and Juristic Persons

The law works by accommodating new activities to old principles, by putting new wine in old bottles. It is for this reason that the law found it convenient to consider corporations as "juristic persons." It could thereby, with some modification, apply to corporations the same laws that pertain to persons, and until forced to do otherwise, consider corporations to have the same rights and obligations before the law as natual persons. In some respects, this way the law works is unfortunate, because it must then engage in continual revisions to catch up with social events, often operating with a set of principles appropriate to an earlier time. To be specific: because the corporation has been viewed as a juristic person, and because the average size and resources of juristic persons relative to the natural persons has continually grown, the law has been slow to recognize power differences between corporations and natural persons. Thus a symmetric allocation of rights between corporations and persons can lead in practice to an asymmetric realization of interests. The exam-

[14] It is not clear whether full nationalization of business corporations, leaving other corporate actors in a society free, would allow sufficient countervailing corporate power to remain in the society to enable persons to successfully oppose the power of the state. Chile will constitute a valuable case for study of this question.

ple of universities and applicants discussed earlier illustrates
this well: a university and an applicant have equal rights
in the transaction, but the power disparity between them
leads to an unequal realization of interests, because the university as the more powerful controls the conditions of the
transaction.

Quite generally, then, a major step toward restitution of
resources from corporate actors to persons would consist in
an explicit recognition by the law of the power disparities
that can exist due to size differences between juristic persons
and natural persons. This would require either an explicit
unbalancing of rights, in order to balance the realization of
interests among unequal parties, or else somewhat more direct intervention of the law into the exercise of rights. Some
of the ways the latter might occur will be indicated shortly.
Some of the former have already occurred in the shift of the
law away from the principle of *caveat emptor*, which was
appropriate when buyer and seller were of similar size and
had relatively equal control over the conditions of the transaction. Now the law supports in a number of ways the rights
of the buyer to be protected from the misuse of power by
the seller.

Market Power and Organizational Power

As suggested in the examples I have given, there appear
to be two types of situations in which persons find themselves
vis-à-vis corporate actors to which they have given resources.
One is the situation in which either in principle or in practice
they may withdraw their resources from the corporate actor
and invest them in another without cost. This is the case of
the competitive market; and in this case, equity is achieved
simply by assuring that he has as much control over the information conditions surrounding the relationships as does
the corporate actor, to insure that his choice serves his interests. His power exercised in this way may be termed mar-

ket power; and it equals that of the corporate actor when he is as fully in control of the conditions surrounding the relationship as is the corporate actor. This situation can be achieved by the investor of capital in the corporation, or by its customer, or by the applicant to a college, or by the family applying to a school under a voucher scheme. It does not exist, however, even as a possibility, for a worker vis-à-vis his union or his employer, for a child in a fixed-district public school system, for a resident of a city, or for a citizen of a state. Those examples illustrate the second type of situation, in which a person cannot withdraw, except at some cost. In that case, he cannot exercise control over the corporate actor by his market choice; he must exercise that control through his control of the actions of the corporate actor itself. As I have indicated earlier, this depends on the possibility of organizing other corporate actors—coalitions, political parties, ad hoc organizations—that can exercise countervailing power in the collective decisions of the corporate actor itself. Such power may be described as organizational power.

For the first of these two situations, it appears that the major benefit accruing to the corporate actor due to its size is its control of information. Thus to bring about equity for persons requires attention to information rights.

Market Power and Information Rights

In a transaction between a corporate actor and a person, the fact that the corporate actor controls much of the information surrounding the transaction is ordinarily ignored by law. This occurs because of the general presumption in law that two persons with equal rights engaging voluntarily in a transaction have equal possibilities of realizing their interests in it. Three examples from those discussed above, however, show how this is not true, due to control by the corporate actor of information surrounding the transaction: universities and applicants, schools under a voucher system, and corporations, with market research and advertising. If there is to be equal realization of interests in such cases, there must be equal rights of access to information. Detailed attention to the types of information surrounding a transaction would be necessary to establish the appropriate legal conditions for such rights. The principle is clear, however: that for any transaction, of the total amount of resources devoted to information surrounding the transaction, half should be under the control of each party to the transaction. This could mean either of two things: that the two parties jointly control the information content, determining through a collective decision the information to be made available to each; or that each party receive half the resources devoted to information, to be used independently. To use the university admissions example, the latter would mean that when a student is required to provide information to colleges, half the total information fee should be allocated to a fund to be used by an applicants' agent to provide applicants with information about colleges and universities. To use the business corporation example, it means that every dollar spent on advertising and market research would be matched by a dollar, similarly taken from sales revenue, to be spent by a customers' agent in providing information of interest to consumers.

Such a proposal may appear unrealistic, and unless implemented with extreme care, could hardly be successful. Obviously, in a consumer market, some set of consumers' agents would have to come into existence in order to use the resources affectively. These would constitute new corporate actors to satisfy interests of consumers, and would, of course, carry with them the danger to persons' interests that all corporate actors contain. Yet equity in this situation is clear: if the information surrounding a transaction between a corporate actor and a person affects the outcome of that transaction (or in the longer run, the character of the products offered), then equity for persons is realized only when they control half the resources devoted to providing information relevant to the transaction.

Such information rights, to be effective, must necessarily be instituted by law. Such legal changes would not constitute a removal of rights from corporate actors per se, for the corporate actors have gained their present control of information through their size and sometimes the power of oligopoly. They would merely constitute a more careful attention to insuring that rights are in fact equal when the parties are of disparate size.

Organizational Power

It is less clear just what modification of existing corporate rights would bring restitution in situations that require use of organizational power. One curious fact, however, gives a possible hint: in the U.S., both stockholders' opposition to management and union members' opposition to incumbent officers were more frequent and more successful in the second half of the 1960s than in the preceding years.[15] These changes could be merely manifestations of the generally increased levels of activism during that period. But they could also be due to an increase in the ease of communication, reducing the information monopoly that the corporation and the union have had vis-à-vis their stockholders or members.[16] If the latter is the case, it suggests that for organizational power as well as market power, information rights are the most important rights to effect restitution. What would appear to be necessary is the existence of parallel channels of communication to enable persons who have invested resources in in the corporation (owners, members, etc.) to hear

[15] I am grateful to S.M. Lipset for pointing out to me the recent increase in union members' opposition to officers.

[16] In this connection, it is interesting to note that in a number of large business corporations, underground newspapers have begun to appear.

opposing positions.[17] Again, these appear to be in the form of information rights for persons. Such information rights, in order to be effective, must exist in law, in the very charter of corporate actors themselves. It is far from clear just how these rights might be expressed, nor is it known how large the corporation can be before such rights are necessary. However, what is important to recognize is the principle: if the corporate actor is not to alienate power from sovereign persons, then its rights must be highly circumscribed as it grows in size. It appears that one of the most important rights of persons to be protected is information rights, whether the person is in a position to exercise market power by a possible withdrawal from the corporate actor, or is restricted to the exercise of organizational power, through control over corporate actions.

A Bill of Rights for Members of Corporate Actors

Because the state charters those corporate actors which have a legal personality, it can—and does—establish their rights as actors in society. Thus it is possible, if explicit and careful attention is given to the details, to establish in the charter itself a bill of rights for persons who invest sovereignty in a corporate actor. Although charters currently do so in small ways, they are relatively naïve concerning questions of power differentials due to size, and in general employ the principle of laissez faire. An explicit bill of rights in a charter would concern itself primarily with internal procedures designed to control the corporate actor and provide weapons to the person to counter the corporate actor's size. I will mention two such possibilities, to give an idea of the direction that such procedures might take.

Adversary procedures / One of the most important safe-

17 In the larger society, for the state as a corporate actor, proposals have been made to provide explicitly parallel and equal communication channels, through free television time for incumbent and opposition; but these have not yet been successful.

guards to persons, protecting them from the power of the state as corporate actor, is the judicial system. And one of the most important elements of the judicial system is the adversary procedure. When interests of two parties are in conflict, the adversary procedure provides supports for each of those interests, in the form of lawyers whose interests are aligned with those of their clients, and a formal setting in which the interests are brought into confrontation.

Corporate actors within the state are not required to have such procedures, though similar procedures have evolved in some. Grievance procedures for workers in industry have similarities to a judicial adversary procedure. General Motors, which is very powerful in relation to each of its dealers, developed rights of appeal for the dealer when a franchise was terminated, as a way of redressing that power equity. This right for auto dealers subsequently did become a provision of law in at least one state, Rhode Island (Berle, 1954, pp. 77–82).

The power and size of corporate actors within modern society, and the amount of sovereignty that persons have invested in these corporate actors (and cannot easily withdraw), imply that such adversary procedures are necessary within corporate actors just as for the state as a whole. The form they should take is not clear, nor is it clear just what kind of a general principle could be incorporated into a charter bill of rights. But the necessity for such a right is clear in those corporate actors from which persons cannot withdraw without costs.

Variation in voting procedures / A vote for a representative is not the only way a member of a corporate body can control and guide his representative. Nor is the use of representatives required to bypass communication difficulties of the sort that once existed (though their use may be valuable for certain other purposes, such as vote bargaining). It would be possible to have a variety of control mechanisms, some of which might provide more protection for persons than do usual voting systems. Two things are necessary in such an alternative system, given that a relatively small fraction of a person's attention is ordinarily devoted to that corporate actor. One is a mechanism to bring to his attention, at low attention-cost to him, those actions of the corporate actor that may affect his interest; and the second is a mechanism for efficiently and accurately using that attention to implement his interests.

Voting systems, or systems by which members can exercise voice, of very different sorts from those currently in existence have been proposed. Instant electronic voting, by which members could register a preference or a vote on any issue, is quite conceivable. Also conceivable is a system by which members receive a regular "income" of votes to distribute as they liked (or withhold) for their representatives of executives, and which the representatives would use in turn as currency in their votes on bills (Coleman, 1971).[18]

The point I want to make here is not to specify just what form such a system of membership control might take, but only to indicate that alternatives *are* possible, and that an analysis of the internal political process of corporate actors can help show what alternatives can provide the greatest restitution of power to persons.

I have tried in this chapter merely to give a glimpse of some of the means by which restitution of power from corporate actors to individuals can occur. If a market in which the corporate actor is involved is highly competitive, then that competition per se takes away the corporate actor's power vis-à-vis those persons it faces in the market. One general set of procedures for restitution, then, is mechanisms

[18] A very early example of alternative ways in which members can exercise a voice is the *Cahiers de Doléances* of 1789 preceding the French Revolution. These were written documents expressing grievances and demands, formulated in each estate in each locality for transmission to the king.

to reduce corporate actors' power to shape the market into noncompetitive forms, through explicit "information rights" provided for persons in such markets.

But not all restitutions can occur in this way. Some must come through explicit means of organizational control of corporate actors by those with investments in it. These means, which could be contained in a corporate "bill of rights" in the corporation's charter, includes things as diverse as adversary procedures and modified voting systems.

4

LEARNING TO LIVE WITH
NEW PERSONS

I<small>T MAY OR MAY NOT BE TRUE</small> that the poor will always be with us; but it is certainly true that corporate actors will. They may take different forms; they may be closed and all encompassing, as in medieval society, or subordinate to the encompassing corporate actor, the state, as in socialist states, or free, as in liberal democracies, the "new corporate actors." But they are always with us, and they will always have power, that is, some ability to implement their interests vis-à-vis individuals.

Consequently, it is important to ask ourselves just how we, as natural persons, can come to live more satisfactorily in a society that contains in it these juristic persons as well. It can partly be done by restricting the rights of corporate actors. But restrictions of rights are of limited value, because it is these very same corporate actors which are *our* instruments to better realize our interests, both material and otherwise. It is necessary to recognize the presence of powerful new persons in the household, and decide how to modify our existence so that it will be more satisfactory in the presence of these new persons than it was in their absence—and not less satisfactory, as it could well be.

Perhaps the matter can best be seen by means of a simple diagram. If it is reasonable to think of two kinds of actors in society, corporate actors and persons, then it follows that there are three kinds of relations or transactions between two parties: one between two persons; one between a person and a corporate actor; and one between two corporate actors. These are labeled 1, 2, and 3 in the diagram below. Relations of type 2 contain two types of actions: action of a person toward a corporate actor, labeled 2a in the diagram, and action of a corporate actor toward a person, labeled 2b.

SECOND PARTY *(object of action)*

FIRST PARTY *(actor)*		PERSON	CORPORATE ACTOR
	Person	1	2a
	Corporate Actor	2b	3

Most of the activities around which society has been organized assume relations only of type 1. For example, schools and families as socializing institutions primarily socialize persons toward successful functioning in relations with other persons, and neglect almost completely their functioning in relations with corporate actors. Dewey's ideas, for example, of "bringing the community into the school," conceived of the community as a set of face-to-face relations between persons. The idea of functioning in a role in a bureaucracy, or arranging for service from the electric company, of knowing how to get action quickly from a city department, or even knowing what services are available, or managing the use of credit when retail firms offer attractive and tantalizing credit possibilities, is something almost absent from elementary and secondary education.

Not only in socializing institutions, but elsewhere as well, there is little cognizance of relations involving corporate actors, and little understanding of how to deal with corporate actors. For example, Richard Hoggart (1970), in his perceptive study, *The Uses of Literacy*, showed an interesting and distressing transformation that had taken place among the lower working classes in an industrial city in the Midlands in England. He shows how, in an earlier period, the norms of behavior, the style of life, the conceptions of what is right and desirable, were generated locally, by norms established through day-to-day interaction among neighbors. Whatever might be said of those norms, they were grounded in the daily experience of persons, in the societal wisdom which comes from living with the consequences of actions over a long period of time. But with the advent of the mass media, there was a strong and continuous invasion into the neighborhood of pseudoexperience created by the mass media, or experiences from very different groups, filtered and distorted by the mass media. What is especially interesting about this is that the new norms, the new styles of life seen to be desirable, were the *incidental* result of actions of the mass media in pursuit of their own interests, moving toward their own goals. What is distressing is the fact that though the impact on the neighborhood was incidental to the mass media, it was indeed great, and persons in the neighborhood had no effective means of controlling it. In this case what had happened was a shift from relations of type 1, between persons, to relations of type 2, between a person and a corporate actor, with primarily actions of type 2b, from the corporation to the person.

In effect, what has happened can be compared to an ocean which had at one time been wholly inhabited by minnows, and had developed patterns of activity based on relations among these minnows, and among schools of minnows. Then, over a period of time, new forms of life emerged, until the ocean was filled with fish of many different kinds and sizes, ranging from minnow to whale. A whole new set of rules of the game, of ways of behaving, of expectations become necessary if the minnows are to continue to find the ocean a good place to be. I want, in this chapter, to discuss what some of those new things should be.

Relations Between the Two Kinds of Persons

As there have come to be the new persons in society, the corporate actors, certain kinds of preferences and favoritism have begun to arise. These can be summed up by saying that each type of person seems to give preferential treatment to its own kind. Natural persons seem to prefer natural persons to corporate actors, and corporate actors seem to prefer corporate actors to natural persons. There are many indicators of both of these things, and I will give only a few examples.

The odd-numbered examples show preferences of persons for persons, and the even-numbered ones show preferences of corporate actors for corporate actors.

1. Juries, made up of natural persons, award higher liability claims when the claims are against a corporation than when they are against an individual.[1]

2. Newspapers, as corporate actors, have been confronted with demands from persons that they publish price comparisons between different food stores, i.e., other corporate actors, to benefit persons. The newspapers have failed to do so, because it would go against the interests of the food stores.

3. Militancy of workers, and general conflict with management, is least in very small shops operated by the proprietor, and increases as the plant becomes larger and the firm takes on the impersonal attributes of a corporate actor. Persons, in their activities as workers, prefer to work for an identifiable person with whom they have some contact, rather than for a corporate actor which acts through agents in positions or offices.

4. Most corporations can get preferences of various sorts from other corporations, relative to individuals: lower interest rates for borrowing, discounts on retail purchases, better service from other corporations. As an example of the last, a telephone call to a business or public administrative office will receive much greater attention when made from another office, i.e., from a person in his capacity as agent of a corporation, than when made by that same person in his private capacity as a natural person. These preferences are often rationally based: the corporate actor ordinarily stands to

[1] I have not gone into detail in the definition of a corporate actor, but a jury may be regarded alternatively as a corporate body acting as agent of the state, or as a set of persons embodying the multiplicity of interests that may be found in plaintiff and defendant, and thus able to weigh those interests in themselves. If regarded in the former way, juries can be seen as corporate actors made up of persons relatively unsocialized into the role of agent of the state, and with no incentive to act as the agent of the state, and thus still acting largely from the perspective of persons.

gain more from a transaction with another corporate actor than from one with a person. But the rational basis makes the preference no less real in its consequences for persons.[2]

5. Many persons (though not all) will do some shopping at small retail stores which are operated by the proprietor, despite an economic loss in doing so because of higher prices. Their stated reasons for doing so focus around "personal attention," "warmth," "friendliness" of the proprietor and his few employees, contrasted with the "coldness," "impersonality," "indifference" of clerks in a large chain store. Such preferences in shopping have not been sufficient to overcome the economic costs of shopping in small retail stores, so that such stores have declined in number; but the continued existence of some in the face of such costs indicates the existence of the preference.

6. Corporate actors of many forms—business firms, trade unions, professional associations, local and state government agencies—will sell to other corporate actors lists of names of persons and their addresses. These lists are used primarily for mail advertising, with the mail sent to the person named on the list provided by one corporate actor to another. In principle, the lists are also available to persons, but their costs are too great for most persons' level of resources, and they are of little use to persons. Mailing lists are only one of many examples of business services provided by corporate actors which are available only to those who have a higher level of resources than most persons, and thus in practice, only to corporate actors. Credit ratings are another widespread example.

7. Most persons are far more interested in news events about persons than about corporate actors. The newspaper

[2] The case is similar to that of policemen who are more suspicious of a young black man than an old white woman, and treat him less well: the suspicion is rationally based, because of the greater probability that he is engaged in a criminal action. But the rational basis does not change the consequences as they are experienced by young black men not engaged in crime.

with largest total circulation in the world is the British *News of the World*. The American largest-circulation paper is the New York *Daily News*. The single most distinguishing feature about these newspapers is their focus upon personal events, such as murders, divorces, reconciliations, personal conflicts, "personal advice" columns, as well as a general personalization of the news. The wide circulations of these papers are merely surface indicators of the far greater interest of persons in other persons than in corporate actors.

8. Corporate actors are favored over natural persons in many ways by governments, which are also corporate actors. Without analyzing the lobbying and other influence processes that allow corporate actors to receive preferential treatment from corporate actors, we can merely observe that in numerous areas, corporations receive preferential treatment. Income tax policy is a good example: corporations have expenses of all types subtracted from their income, and only the resulting difference is taxed. Persons, in contrast, have all their income taxed, despite the fact that obviously a large portion of it is merely expenses in the same sense that the corporation has expenses. Some persons find that they can gain income tax benefits by incorporating themselves, in effect pretending before the tax law to be a corporation, in order to receive the additional benefits that accrue to corporations. Regulatory agencies constitute another example: acting as agents of the state, and ordinarily set up as agencies to protect the interests of persons in transactions with corporations, they have often functioned instead to protect the corporations' interests.

These examples could be extended indefinitely. Each can be explained or accounted for in some way, but they add up to the two broad generalizations stated earlier: persons give preferential treatment to other persons, and corporate actors give preferential treatment to other corporate actors. Relations of types 1 and 3 in the diagram appear to be self-consistent, each part of a system of relationships between one kind of entity. In the first, persons establish a relation as persons, between themselves, in joint or complementary activities that are directly relevant to their goals as persons. In the type 3 relation, persons engage in an interaction only as agents of corporate actors. The activities of the interaction are directly relevant to the goals of the corporate actors they represent. The activities are extrinsic to their personal goals, and only indirectly affect them.

But in a relation of type 2, there is a crossover between two systems, the system of personal relations, and the system of relations among corporate actors. It may be an action of a person toward the property of a corporate actor, or interaction between a person and an agent of a corporate actor. If it is the latter, superficial observation would not distinguish it from an interaction between two persons. It is, however, a relation between a person and an agent. For the person, the activities of the interaction are directly relevant to his goals as a person; the relation is intrinsically important to him. For the agent, however, this is not so; the activities are directly relevant to the corporate actor's goal, and only indirectly so to his own.

The consequences of this mismatch are several and serious. The agent's interest in the activities of the interaction is only a derived interest, its strength depending on how tightly the corporate actor has tied its agent's personal goals to the corporate goals.[3] The ties are ordinarily not a direct linking of corporate and personal goals, but involve a contingency in which personal interests, such as salary increases or keeping the job, are to some degree tied to achievement of corporate goals. In general, these ties are not extremely tight, and as a result, the agent is far less involved in the relation

[3] Corporate actors do this differentially well for different of their agents. Salesmen on commission have their personal goals directly tied to the corporate goal. But ordinarily, agents who provide services that are not directly paid for by a customer do not have their personal goals so closely tied to the corporate actor's, and are thus far less deeply involved in the relation than is the person.

than is the person. The effects of this on the relation can be very strong. The inattention or poor service of clerks, the carelessness of workers, the discourtesy of government bureaucrats are all results of the weak tie between corporate goals and those of the agent.

These relationships of type 2, which cross the boundary between two systems of relations, constitute the weakest and most defective link in the structure of which modern society consists. The defects are on both sides of the relation, on the side of persons and on the side of agents of corporate actors. I will look at some of the defects on the personal side first. The first of these leads us back to Kant's categorical imperative.

Normative Systems and Kant's Categorical Imperative

Immanuel Kant, as a moral philosopher, was concerned with developing a prescriptive law as a first principle of a social order, a law the obedience to which would insure the proper functioning of the social order. The law which he derived is his famous categorical imperative: "Act only on that maxim [i.e., subjective principle of action] through which you can will that it should become a universal law" (Paton, 1948, p. 84).

Kant's categorical imperative is of special intellectual interest in that it does not prescribe the *content* of principles of morality, but only the *process* by which that content is to be decided. The process depends on the explicit separation of man into different selves: the acting self and the self as judge of action—a division which, along with the self as object of action, was earlier stated by Adam Smith.[4] In this

---

[4] A different distinction between two selves is made explicitly by Kant at another point (Paton, 1948, p. 116). The distinction is between the self as intelligence and a free will, and the self as a natural being, subject to natural laws of cause and effect. But this distinction is a different one, introduced by Kant to resolve the paradox of free will in a natural world of cause and effect.

process of deciding what actions are to be allowed, Kant provides a neat solution to the intellectual problem of a self-regulating social system. The solution consists of a regulator or governor at each of the multiple centers of action of which individual persons consist, but a governor different from the one which was first described by the utilitarian political philosophers. In the utilitarian theory, each person is guided by self-interest and limited only by self-interest (and by the constraints imposed by others' pursuit of their interests), and the system of action consists of a system of tension between actors whose interests lie in different directions. But in Kant's system, each actor, though self-interested, is limited in pursuit of those interests by the other aspect of his self: the judging self, whose governing principles do not depend on the particular standpoint of the acting self, but should ideally be the same from actor to actor. The judging self surveys the social system from a perspective different from that of the acting self, including the perspective of those potential objects of the action contemplated by the acting self. Kant's imperative becomes a dressed-up and sophisticated version of the Golden Rule, "Do unto others as you would have them do unto you."

Although Kant goes beyond the utilitarians in stating a categorical imperative as a moral law one must obey regardless of his personal interests, the *practice* of this law can in many conditions be derived from utilitarian principles. That is, when an actor is acting toward a person like himself, he sees himself as a potential recipient of the consequences of his action. Those anticipated consequences will lead him to act in a way that appears to follow Kant's moral law. However, he follows it not through direct application of this moral law, but through recognition of the consequences such an action could have for him when he is in that situation.

In stable egalitarian communities where actions are face-to-face transactions between persons, these conditions hold reasonably well for most actions. Natural limits are imposed on the exercise of self-interest by the recognition that one is himself sometime likely to be in a position comparable to that of the person who is the object of his contemplated action. In modern society, however, one condition in particular has changed this: the existence of corporate actors with whom persons engage in transactions. The change occurs in two ways: in the actions of agents of corporate actors, and in the actions of persons toward corporate actors.

To consider the latter first: if a person carries out an action toward another person, he is carrying out an action toward another actor like himself. The other actor can be expected to respond in kind, subject to the resources he holds. But if the first actor carries out an action toward a large corporate actor, there are several differences. First, that actor is very likely never to know who carried out the action. For example, destruction of another person's property is ordinarily detectable, because the other person, about the same size as the first, sequesters his property closely about him, and pays attention to it. (If his property is vast, then he ordinarily operates as a corporate actor, with several agents.) But destruction of a corporate actor's property often is not observable: a public telephone can be ripped from the wall without detection by interested parties.

A second and more important difference is that the corporate actor often cannot respond individually toward actions of individual persons. Thus only when shoplifting in a department store reaches a certain magnitude is it economically feasible for the store to provide security persons to apprehend shoplifters. The phenomenon is a special case of the general phenomenon that economists call a "free rider." When an action is being carried out by a large actor on a mass basis, that actor cannot modify his action to fit the details of a transaction with each of the many persons it does business with.

More centrally related to the categorical imperative,

when a person acts toward another person, he can see himself in the other's place. Thus he is motivated to act according to Kant's categorical imperative, though perhaps in reality on grounds of long-range self-interest. However, when he carries out an action toward a corporate actor, he cannot see himself ever in the corporate actor's place. He will never become a corporate actor. For that reason, he will feel fewer pangs of guilt when he rips out a public telephone or steals paper from the office than he would if he had committed similar acts against a person.

From the person's standpoint, then, the rational self-interested basis for obedience to Kant's categorical imperative is undermined at this boundary between systems of personal relations and systems of corporate actor relations. The supports for a normative system have been taken away.

From the corporate actor's standpoint also, the rational basis for obedience to Kant's categorical imperative is gone in type 2 relations. For the corporate actor will never be a person, and thus need not look at a contemplated corporate action through the eyes of the person who receives its consequences. Thus a bank as a corporation can foreclose a mortgage much more quickly and easily than can a banker who knows something about the person who is subject to foreclosure. Or a city school system can expel students or carry out other disciplinary actions of far greater harm to a child than the physical punishment the child once took at the hands of a schoolmaster—because the school system will never be in the position of an expelled child. It is easy for a person to be an "administrative casualty" of a corporate actor of some sort, a person to whom injustice has been done not by intent, but because of the insensitivity of corporate actors to persons.

Such failure on the part of corporate actors to put themselves in the position of persons affected by their actions is not merely due to the fact that they are corporate actors. For those who make such decisions as agents of the corporate actor are in fact persons, who could put themselves in the position of other persons, and thus soften or humanize the action. But a frequent property of large corporate actors is that they have complex internal structure, so that the implementation of the action is by a *different* agent from the one who decided the policy, perhaps far removed from him in the organizational structure. The corporate structure does not easily and sensitively transmit from implementing agent to policy-maker the effects on persons of a corporate action. Both failures in *communication* among the different agents of a corporate actor and gaps between different agents in *responsibility* reduce the effectiveness of this transmission.[5]

Thus the rational basis for Kant's imperative is undermined on the corporate actor's side because its structure makes it insensitive to the consequences of its actions for persons. It is true, of course, that persons can and do organize to make their interests felt by a corporate actor. But in systems that are wholly built on personal relations, these interests are anticipated and reacted to in anticipation, obeying to some extent Kant's moral law, and giving these systems a less polarized and more dampened confrontation of interests.

Altogether, a portion of the rational basis for a moral system is cut away where persons and corporate actors must coexist. The immediate question is: What can replace it? But the answer is not so immediate. The difficulties appear inherent in the differences between corporate actor and person. Two paths seem possible. The first is to give persons more of the characteristics of corporate actors or at least greater understanding of corporate actors. The second is to modify the structure of corporate actors to give them more of the qualities of persons.

[5] Sasha Wietman suggests also that the agent's necessity to justify his actions within the corporate actor makes him less sensitive to the interests of the person than would be the case if he were not merely an agent, but the actor in a transaction.

Changing Natural Persons

The change in persons depends principally on patterns of socialization. It is a change that probably can be carried out only if children experience much more fully than they do at present a wide range of activities in which they are agents of corporate actors. Or, as sociologists would describe it, if they participate much earlier in formal bureaucratic organizations with a structure of role relations rather than personal relations. This might be described loosely as earlier and more systematically designed exposure to the "cold, impersonal world." This exposure would replace the naïve and personalistic idealism (which is ordinarily shattered within a few years, sometimes with bad psychological consequences for the person) with a more calculating, strategic, even Machiavellian approach to the world. Such socialization occurs to some extent merely through life in an urban area, rather than a rural one; nevertheless, many children in urban areas are well shielded from any but face-to-face personal relations. My suggestion here is that this shielding is harmful for the child who must later live in a society filled with corporate actors.

The socialization task implied by the social structure of the modern world involves learning all the different modes of relation to corporate actors. These include both long-term contractual relations and short-term transactions. Of the former, there are two principal types of relation. The first is that of an owner, member, investor, a person who invests resources in a corporate actor with the aim of realizing benefits from it. The second is that of employee or agent, who contracts to give his personal services to the corporate actor in return for compensation, ordinarily money, from the corporate actor. The short-term transactions with corporate actors involve both those which occur in a market structure (ordinarily as a customer), and those which occur outside a market structure (as a client of the school system, police department, telephone company, welfare department, etc.).

The learning necessary for all these different types of relation to corporate actors encompasses a wide number of things. No curriculum has been designed to systematically provide such learning; but if a person is to be able to responsibly satisfy his interests in type 2 relations in modern society, a curriculum of such scope is necessary.

Changing Corporate Actors

The second path is a change in corporate actors to give them more of the qualities of persons. This path can include several kinds of changes. Five aspects of modern corporate actors which make transactions with them difficult for persons have been mentioned in earlier sections. One of these is the large size of many corporate actors. In Chapter 3, some ways of reducing the size—and thus power—disparity between persons and corporate actors were discussed, and those will not be repeated here. The other four are (1) the narrow and single-focused interests or goals of corporate actors in comparison to persons' multiplicity of goals; (2) their imperfect communication structure; (3) the gaps that exist in their structure of responsibility, with some events falling between the realms of responsibility of different positions; and (4) the imperfect connection between the agent's interest and that of the corporate actor, making him less involved and interested than the person in a successful outcome of the transaction between agent and person.

It is possible to modify each of these five aspects of a corporate actor, and some such modifications might create a variety of corporate actor which would be more compatible with persons than are present corporate actors constructed on a bureaucratic model. Corporate actors in society have been in a continual state of evolution, and just as new forms evolved with the decline of the Middle Ages, new forms may evolve today. I will mention examples of modifications in each of these areas.

First, the single-purposedness of modern corporate actors has the consequence of focusing the activities of its employees (or agents) on a single set of goals, those involving the production of certain goods or services—private goods and services in the case of business corporations, public goods and services in the case of government, and some mixtures of these in other kinds of corporate actors. In doing so, however, in contracting for the services of its agents, it has insulated them from the "dependent" segments of society: the young, the old, the sick, the disabled. Before this insulation existed, the burdens of such dependency were intermixed with work, and shared by all, in activities incidental to work. The existence of the insulation, in the form of bureaucratic work organizations, has taken the time and attention of the self-sufficient away from the vicinity of the dependent, and prevented the latter from depending personally and directly on the former. The dependency has become indirect, through the purchase of care in institutions: in nurseries, day-care centers, schools, hospitals, old-age homes. The defects of many of those institutions as general dependent-care institutions have become evident in recent years, raising questions about whether this structure is better than the incidental dependency care that once existed outside modern corporate actors in families and neighborhoods.

The possible modification of modern corporate actors would involve explicit introduction of dependent persons into them, with care incidentally being provided by the full-time employees of the corporate actor. Such an arrangement would require subsidy from the body ultimately responsible for the dependent person (the state or the family), and the care would constitute an additional goal for the corporate actor—giving it a greater variety of goals than it presently has.

Such changes in corporate actors could probably occur most readily for schoolchildren, coming into a greatly modified business office or plant, and indeed, movements in this direction exist in a number of countries.[6] But what remains is to provide both the design and the incentives for the development of such diversified corporate actors.

The imperfect communication in corporate actors can only be remedied by change in the structure of organizations, making them more able to transmit with full sensitivity and without loss of information the experiences of an *implementing* agent to the *policy-making agent*. This may be accomplished by reducing information loss of all links in that structure or by reducing the structural distance between policy-maker and implementing agent. The latter is in effect decentralization of policy-making. Thus if the above arguments are valid, decentralization of decision-making in a corporate actor will make it more like a person in its reactions to persons. This does not mean it will be kinder or more beneficent, because some persons are cruel, some are selfish, and most are self-interested. It means that the corporate actor will be less insensitive to the impact of its actions on persons, and will be less likely to lose them or make of them administrative casualties because of communication failures within the corporate actor.

The gaps in responsibility within corporate actors also require some kind of structural change. When clients of a corporate actor are handed from one agent to another over the telephone or in the office, such responsibility gaps frequently occur. The person becomes an administrative casualty because one agent withdraws responsibility before another accepts it, letting the client's problem slip through. Some form of organization that had built-in overlap of responsibility would, at the expense of some redundancy of effort, close up the responsibility gap and make the corporate

---

[6] See Coleman (1972) for a discussion of this kind of change in corporations.

actor more like a single-bodied person. Precisely how this might occur remains for experimentation to assess; but the requirements are clear. In corporate actors that produce products and those which give services, there has been some effort in this direction, with procedures that require the agent to identify himself by name in providing the service or to have his name attached to the product. There has been, in effect, a legal "limited liability" of the agent in transactions where he represents the corporate actor; some increase in that liability might provide the necessary incentive for the necessary assumption of responsibility by agents.

There may also be imperfect connection in a transaction involving an agent and a person, between the corporate actor's goal and the agent's goal. These make the agent unresponsive to the person's actions, and lead him to treat the transaction as a routine case without attention to its details. Numerous efforts have been devoted to creating appropriate incentives for agents, individual and group, to tie more closely corporate goals to personal goals of the agent. Beyond noting that work has been done in this direction, I will not examine this problem further.

There are many examples in modern society that show the breakdown of relations between corporate actors and persons due to the gulf that separates the characteristics of persons and the characteristics of corporate actors. One sociological study that illustrates this very well is a paper by Katz and Eisenstadt (1960) which describes the confrontation in Israel between Eastern Jews and the state bureaucracy. This confrontation is in effect a confrontation between a system of relations between persons (with the family as the basic unit), and a social system containing many modern corporate actors. The behavior of persons unfamiliar with the person-agent relation shows several interesting characteristics. First, the clients of a state bureaucracy expect to establish a direct relation with the agent; expect the agent to give personal attention to their problem, even if his assignment changes. They expect to be able to get special benefits from the state agency through "knowing someone," that is, through a personal relation with someone inside the agency. The attempts to develop these personal connections are widespread, and have had a serious impact on the bureau-cratic rationality and even-handedness of the agencies.[7]

On the corporate actor's side in this same case, the defects in the behavior of the agent show one dominant characteristic that exemplifies the problem of agent unresponsiveness dis-cussed earlier: the agents show some degree of indifference to the demands or interests of the person. This may take the form of lack of continuity in the relation. The Eastern Jewish client of a state agency, for example, is puzzled when he is handed from one agent to another to another, with no con-tinuity of relation to any one person. It is also true that de-pending on the incentive structure in the corporate actor, a "difficult case" (which gives few rewards and many prob-lems) may be passed on endlessly from one agent to another, like a hot potato from hand to hand.

This example shows some of the special difficulties in-volved at the borderline between the two types of relational systems—a borderline which is crossed by type 2 relations between person and corporate actor. To explicate these diffi-culties is not to solve them; but it indicates the kind of mech-anisms that are necessary to overcome them.

Loss of Control and Contracted Horizons

There is one more question important to address in learn-ing to live in a society filled with corporate actors. This is a psychological question: How can persons in society regain

---

[7] The fact that a corporate actor becomes less universalistic, more dependent on personal relations does not necessarily mean that it is less beneficial for persons. For an even-handed and fair indifference may be less beneficial than an interested but unfair system. Such questions need much more empirical study.

a sense of control, and overcome the sense of powerlessness that large corporate actors induce?

I discussed some of the ways this might be done in the preceding chapter, by examining how there might be restitution of power to persons. But such restitution is limited because of the very benefits that large corporate actors bring, benefits that most persons are not willing to forego.

There is one other way a person can regain a sense of control. This is to withdraw, to reduce the scope of one's horizons. It is to limit one's interest in and attention to those events that are very near at hand, and subject to one's own control, or at least influence.

I suspect that in the long run some such solution may be necessary for most persons. For the mass media continually expand our horizons and in so doing interest us in events over which we have no control. This should produce, all other things being equal, a slow erosion of a sense of control for most persons. If it does so, the only long-range solution may be to restrict one's attention to matters close at hand, to withdraw attention from distant matters. This involves two changes: a concentration and focusing of interests, rather than a dispersion; and focus upon activities that are close at hand, in the near vicinity, rather than those that are distant.

The communal movement in the United States is interesting from this point of view, because it constitutes one type of withdrawal of attention from distant activities. It explicitly draws in the limits of the relevant events, by cutting itself off from the larger society and focusing attention inward. Without evidence, it would be too conjectural to suggest that the communal movement has been and is an attempt to reinstate a psychological sense of power or control. But the movement does show a possible means by which horizons may be contracted and a sense of control reinstated. The viability of this means is questionable, because communal groups as corporate actors are a more primitive form of social organization than are modern corporate actors, wholly containing their members. They are like medieval corporate bodies in this, though the internal structure of communes is sometimes egalitarian, in contrast to the hierarchical structure of most medieval corporate bodies. This very egalitarian character can itself create internal organizational problems in communes, because communal bodies require extreme imposition of discipline (often through charismatic authority) to break down the disruptive forces due to special relationships and cliques within the commune.[8]

Even with these problems of communal groups, it may be that some mixed mode of existence may be viable, involving portions of one's time and attention confined within a communal group, and portions lived in the larger society with its corporate actors, large and small. This would appear to be a violation of the very prerequisites of a communal group, for the group would no longer wholly contain its members. Nevertheless, such a form is beginning to occur in Israeli kibbutzim, and it may show sufficient strength to continue.

In describing some of the changes that can make it possible for persons and corporate actors to live together in peace and equity, I have only begun to open the box of questions, problems, and possibilities. What is necessary is to examine carefully and with empirical research the elements that I have discussed. At this point in history, only a few things are clear: there are two systems of relations coexisting in modern society, there are important problems at their numerous points of contact, and there are ways to reduce the seriousness of these problems. There is the objective fact that persons have lost control over some of the events important to them, there is the subjective fact that distant and distantly controlled events are increasingly important to persons. And there are ways that persons can regain a sense of control.

[8] See Zablocki (1972) for a discussion of the mechanisms of social control in an intentional community.

References

Berle, A. A., *The Twentieth Century Capitalist Revolution* (New York: Harcourt Brace, 1954).

Berle, A. A., and G. C. Means, *The Modern Corporation and Private Property* (New York: Macmillan, 1940).

Coleman, James S., "The Symmetry Principle in College Choice," *College Board Review*, No. 73 (Fall 1969), 5–10.

———. "Loss of Power," *American Sociological Review*, 38 (1973), 1–17.

———. "How Do the Young Become Adults," *Review of Educational Research*, Vol. 42, No. 4 (1972).

Commons, John, *The Legal Foundations of Capitalism* (New York: Macmillan, 1924).

Davis, John P., *Corporations* (New York: Putnam, 1905).

Gierke, Otto von, *Political Theories of the Middle Ages*, trans. by F. W. Maitland, (Cambridge: Cambridge University Press, 1900).

———. *Natural Law and the Theory of Society* (Cambridge: Cambridge University Press, 1934). (First published in German in 1913).

Hayek, F. A. von, "The Corporation in a Democratic Society: In Whose Interest Ought It and Will It Be Run?" in *Management and Corporations 1985*, Melville Anshen and George Leland Bach (New York: McGraw-Hill, 1960).

Hirschman, A. O., *Exit, Voice, and Loyalty: Response to Decline in Firms* (Cambridge: Harvard University Press, 1971).

Hoggart, Richard, *The Uses of Literacy* (Oxford: Oxford University Press, 1970). (First published by Essential Books, 1957.)

Kantorowicz, Ernst H., *The King's Two Bodies* (Princeton: Princeton University Press, 1957).

Katz, E., and S. N. Eisenstadt, "Some Sociological Observations on the Response of Israeli Organizations to New Immigrants," *Administrative Science Quarterly*, 5 (June 1960), 113–33.

Kornhauser, William, *The Politics of Mass Society* (New York: Free Press, 1959).

Lipset, S. M., M. A. Trow, and J. S. Coleman, *Union Democracy* (New York: Free Press, 1956).

Maitland, F. W., *Trust und Korporation* (Vienna: Alfred Holder, 1904).

McPherson, C. B., *The Political Theory of Possessive Individualism: Hobbes to Locke* (Oxford: Oxford University Press, 1962).

Michels, Robert, *Political Parties* (New York: Free Press, 1949).

Paton, H. J., trans., *The Moral Law: Kant's Groundwork of the Metaphysic of Morals* (London: Hutcheson and Co., 1948).

Pollock, F., and F. W. Maitland, *The History of English Law*, Vol. 1, 2nd ed. (Cambridge: Cambridge University Press, 1898).

Preiser, E., "Property and Power in the Theory of Distribution," *International Economic Papers*, No. 2 (1952), 206–20.

Ransford, H. E., "Isolation, Powerlessness and Violence," *American Journal of Sociology*, 73 (1968), 581–91.

Rawls, John, *The Theory of Justice* (Cambridge: Harvard University Press, 1971).

Reich, Charles, "The New Property," *The Public Interest* (1966).

Rotter, Julian B., "External Control and Internal Control," *Psychology Today* (June 1971), 5.

Seale, P., and M. McConville, *French Revolution, 1968* (London: Penguin Books, 1968).

Seeman, M., "Alienation and Social Learning in a Reformatory," *American Sociological Review*, 69 (1963), 270–84.

———. "Alienation, Membership and Political Knowledge," *Public Opinion Quarterly*, 30 (1966), 353–67.

———. "Powerlessness and Knowledge: A Comparative Study of Alienation and Learning," *Sociometry*, 30 (1967), 105–23.

———. "Alienation and Engagement," in A. Campbell and P. E. Converse, eds., *The Human Meaning of Social Change* (New York: Russell Sage, 1971) (a).

———. "The Urban Alienations: Some Dubious Theses from Marx to Marcuse," *Journal of Personality and Social Psychology*, Vol. 19, No. 2 (1971), 135–43 (b).

Ullman, Walter, *The Individual and Society in the Middle Ages* (Baltimore: Johns Hopkins Press, 1966).

Weber, Max, *Law in Economy and Society*, ed. with introduction and annotations by Max Rheinstein (Cambridge: Harvard University Press, 1954).

Weitman, Sasha, "Flags of All Nations," *Semiotica*, in press, 1973.

Zablocki, Benjamin D., *The Joyful Community* (Baltimore: Penguin Books, 1971).

Index

Page numbers in *italics* refer to footnotes.

Active property, 43
Administrative casualty, 97–98, 102–103
Adversary procedure, 81–82
Agents, *see* Employees
Alienation
  of economic power, 44–46
  by organization, 47–49
  of power, 64–67
  from work, 53–54
American College Testing Program, 65
Ascending theory of government, 73
Association, 23

Berle, A. A., 42–46, 58
Berry, George, 48
Bill of rights, 81–84
Body politic
  attribute of King, 19–20
  as Crown, 20
  see also Corporation sole
Bureaucracy
  administrative casualty, 97–98, 103–104
  dealing with, 37–38, 53, 88, 93, 101–104
  decentralization of, 102
  emergence of, 35–37
Burgesses of Nottingham, 18
Burgesses of Retford, 19
Business corporation
  constitutional contracts of, 40, 44–46
  disparity of power, 41, 60–62
  growth of, 15, 27

as juristic persons, 14–15
modification of power, 64–65, 79, 101–102
nationalized, 76
pyramiding, 45, 59
underground newspapers, 80

Cahiers de Doléances, 83
Caveat emptor, 77
Charles I, 20
Charter, *see* Constitutional contract
Chile, 76
Churches, as trust, 22
Citizen, 29, 42–43, 75–76
Coleman, James S., 47, 48, 50, 63, 65, 70, 83, 102
College admissions, 65–67, 72, 79
College Entrance Examination Board, 65–66
"Common school," *see* Public school system
Commons, John, 40
Communal movement, 105–106
Communist Party, 47
Community as a whole, 58
Community control, 70
Conflict of interest
  adversary procedure, 81–82
  between persons, 69
  constitutional contracts, 44
  public schools, 72
Constitutional amendment, 40
Constitutional contract
  alienation of economic power, 44–46
  bill of rights, 81–83

conflict of interest, 44
described, 43–44
majority rule, 38–41
trade union manipulation, 46–50
Consumer, 60–62, 79–80, 91
Contract, *see* Constitutional contract
Corporate actor, *see* Free corporate actor; Juristic persons
Corporate bodies, 14, *15*
Corporation, *see* Business corporation
Corporation sole, 19–22
Countervailing corporation, 62–65, 73, 78
see also Organizational power
Credit ratings, 91
"Cult of unity," 47

Descending theory of government, 73–74
Dewey, John, 88
Duchy of Lancaster, 19

East India Company, 27
Edward IV, 19–20
Eisenstadt, S. M., 103
Elementary and Secondary Education Act, 69
Employees, 36, 99
Exit, *63*
External control, 52

Fictional person, 23
Free corporate actor, 15
see also Juristic persons
Free rider, 96
Free Speech Movement, 53
Free will, *94*

General Motors, 82
Gesellschaft, 23
Gierke, Otto von, *15*, 25–26

Hayek, F. A. von, 59
Hierarchy
accepted attributes, 26
dissolution of, 26–28
medieval political theory, 25–26
Hirschman, A. O., 63
Hobbes, Thomas, 74
Hoggart, Richard, 88–89

Income tax policy, 92
Incorporation, 40, 45
Information rights
market power, 78–81
organizational power, 80
students and, 65–67, 79
transactions, 60–62
voting systems, 83–84
Inter vivos trust, 21
Interests and rights, 15–16
Internal control, 52
International Typographical Union, *63*, 64
Investor, 41, 44–46, 59, 62, 78, 99
see also Sovereigns; Stockholders
"Iron law of oligarchy," 46

Juries, 90
Juristic persons
before the law, 76–77
defined, 14–15
as force in social change, 28, 57
growth as motive, 49, 59
growth of, 14–15, 27, 29–31
interrelationships, 90–94
modification of, 100–103

Kant, Immanuel, 94–98
Kantorowicz, Ernst H., *20*
Katz, E., 103
Kibbutzim, 106
Kings
compared to Pope, 20
concept of "two bodies," 19–20
as corporation sole, 19–20
growth as juristic persons, 19–21
role in social change, 26–28
Kornhauser, William, 50

Labor unions
alienation by organization, 47–49
constitutional contracts of, 46–50
as countervailing corporations, 62–65, 73, 78
"cult of unity," 47
elections, 47–48
information rights, 80–81
International Typographical

Union, *63*, 64
"iron law of oligarchy," 46
militancy in, 90
power disparity, 62–64
powerlessness in, 41–42
Printing Pressmen's Union, 48
Teamsters Union, 50
Laissez faire, 81
Landowner, 16–17
Law
    accommodation by, 76–77
    affected by Roman law, 23
    affected by social change, 13,
        23–25
    and development of juristic
        person, 17–18
    and information rights, 78–81
    as safeguard, 81–82
Liberal democracy, 41, 87
Lipset, S. M., *47, 48, 50, 63, 80*
Locke, John, 74

Machiavellian approach, 99
McPherson, C. B., 74
Mail advertising, 91
Maitland, F. W., *14, 15, 21*
    exceptions to natural persons,
        14
Majority rule, 39–40, *45*, 59
Market power, 60–64, 70–71, 77–
    81
Marx, Karl, 37, *53–54*, 74
Mass media, 51–52, 88–89, 105
"Mass society," 50
Means, G. C., 42–46, 58
Medici bankers, 27
Medieval political theory, 25–26
Melting pot, 67
Members
    benefits as constraints, 49
    as investors, 36, 44, 58–59, 80,
        99
    as students, 65–72
    union power disparity, 62–64
Michels, Robert, 46
Modified voting systems, 82–84
Monopoly, 60–61, 78–80

Natural persons
    affected by communication, 51–
        52, 88–89
    changing, 99–100
    defined, 14

exceptions to, *14*
marginality of, 35–38
role in hierarchy, 25–26
as source of power, 41–43
sovereignty of, 74–75
two selves, 94–98
Natural rights, 28–29, 57, 74
New York *Daily News*, 92
News of the World, 92
Newspapers, 90–92
Nonvoting common stock, 45–46

Obsolescence, 61–62
Oligopoly, 60–66
Organizational power, 38–41, 63–
    64, 78, 80–81
Owners, *see* Members

Parallel interest, 44
Passive property, 43
Paton, H. J., 94
Physical body, 19
Pollock, F., and F. W. Maitland,
    16, 20
Power disparity
    for consumer, 60–62
    for labor, 63–64
    for students, 65–72
Powerlessness
    of citizens, 42–43
    communication as cause of, 50–
        51
    indicated, 48–49, 52, 57
    of investors, 41, 44–46
    of "mass society," 50
    measured, 52
    of owners, 40
    process of, 37–39
    and property rights, 43
    psychic effect of, *53–54*
    of union membership, 41–42,
        46–48
    and violence, 53
Preferred stock, 45
Preiser, E., *61*
Price-fixing, 60
Printing Pressmen's Union, 48
Property rights, 42–43, 73
Proxy vote, 45
Public interest, *58*
Public school system, 67–72, 88
Public servants, *58*

Purpoole, Patrick, *38*
Pyramiding, *45, 59*

Ransford, H. E., 53
Rawls, John, *74*
Reich, Charles, *73*
Rhode Island, 82
Roman law, 23–24
Rotter, Julian B., 52
Rousseau, Jean Jacques, 74

St. Paul, 17
Seale, P., and M. McConville, *53*
Security Council, 40
Seeman, Melvin, 52–53
Smith, Adam, 94
Social Democratic Party, 46
Socialist democracy, 41
Socializing institutions, 87–89
Society
    affected by mass media, 50–51,
        88–89
    breakdown of relations within,
        103–104
    common-sense view of, 13
    as communal groups, 105–106
    feudal structure, 28
    and the law, 13, 76–77
    as "mass society," 50
    as nations, 49
    as organic unit, 25–26
    patterns of socialization, 99
    powerlessness within, 37–38,
        50–53
    public schools and, 67–68
    relationships within, 87–88, 101
    sovereignty, 73
    transformation of, 29–30, 36–37

Sovereigns, 44, 64
    see also Members; Stockholders
Sovereignty, 73–75
Stock, *see* Nonvoting common
    stock; Preferred stock; Stock
    in trust
Stock in trust, 45
Stockholders, 45–46, 59–60, 80
Students
    information rights of, 65–67,
        79
    and public schools, 67–72
    and violence, 53

Teamsters Union, 50
Towns, 18–19
Trade unions, *see* Labor unions
Trow, M. A., *47, 48, 50, 63*
Trust, 21–22
"Two bodies," 19–20

Ullman, Walter, 73
United Nations, 40
United States Constitution, 30
Universitas, 23
Uses of Literacy, The, 88–89
Utilitarian principle, 95

Voice, *63*
Voting system, *see* Modified voting
    systems

Walaszek, Anna, *60*
Weber, Max, *15*, 36
Weitman, Sasha, *49, 98*
Workers' parties, *see* Labor unions

Zablocki, Benjamin D., *106*